Our American warriors are the best the world has ever known; their commitment to being the guardians of our republic is exceptional. However, there are times when these men and women are in need of support. *An Unfair Advantage* is the personal story of one warrior, US Marine Corps Special Operator and Force Reconnaissance member Chad Robichaux. Chad is the pure embodiment of a modern-day Spartan, and he has the résumé to prove it, from the battlefields of Afghanistan to the ring of combat as a mixed martial arts (MMA) champion. However, the outward warrior hid an inner pain, a hurt that could not be filled with the prescriptions of the secular world. Chad tried worldly means to heal himself from post-traumatic stress and failed. This walking man of steel was being weakened by the kryptonite that almost ended his marriage and his life. Then Chad found the real antidote, the power of our Lord and Savior Jesus Christ with whom we can do all things. Chad's victory led him to establish the Mighty Oaks Warrior Foundation that heals warriors with the blessings of allowing Jesus Christ into their lives, and they have not lost a warrior. *An Unfair Advantage* is a must-read to give evidence of the real battle, the unseen enemy our troops face. Yet, regardless, it gives witness that the full armor of God is the best means by which our warriors can win on the spiritual battlefield. It is not about another policy, just trusting in a Savior who has overcome it all (John 16:33).

Allen B. West
Member of the 112th US Congress; US Army Lt. Colonel (Ret.);
Iraq Veteran; Bronze Star Recipient; Author; Fox News Contributor;
Senior Fellow, London Center for Policy Research

An Unfair Advantage is a must-read. I served as a United States marine for 36 years. It was truly an honor to serve with warriors like Chad Robichaux. Chad's personal experience with post-traumatic stress (PTS) after returning from combat is something that many warriors who've seen the "horrors of combat" can relate to. Chad's personal story will touch many warriors experiencing PTS and their families. It is my sincere hope that Chad's story of the power of our Lord and Savior Jesus

Christ, who led him to victory, will touch other great warriors and their families going through the "horrors of combat" and lead them to victory on the spiritual battlefield. Chad's book is an example of Joshua 1:9. "Have I not commanded you? Be strong and courageous. Do not be afraid; do not be discouraged, for the Lord your God will be with you wherever you go." This book will be a blessing to others!

Sergeant Major Carlton Kent
16th Sergeant Major of the US Marine Corps (Ret.); Navy Distinguished Service Medal; Legion of Merit, Bronze Star Recipient

God is the Creator. He made warriors. He made men. He made them with a purpose. If you don't find that purpose you'll be as unfulfilled as if you're trying to use a screwdriver for a shovel or a hammer for a mop. *An Unfair Advantage* helps men and warriors find the very purpose for which they were created.

David Barton, "America's Historian"
Founder & President of WallBuilders; *New York Times* Best-Selling Author, *The Jefferson Lies*; *Time* Magazine's Top 25 Most-Influential Evangelicals

Every boy dreams of being a hero. When boys become men, success is what they pursue while deep down still dreaming of being a hero of noble character. Success often comes at the expense of those things that matter most. Chad's story is not every man's story, but it is a story for every man—a story of success, failure, and, most important, redemption.

Robert "Bill" Coate
USMC Colonel (30 yrs., Ret.); Intelligence Commander and Iraq Veteran; Legion of Merit and Bronze Star Recipient; Author of *You: The Last Best Hope to Restore Our Nation*

Operating from the depths of darkness in enemy territory, a recon marine maneuvers through life's minefields. Ambushes from multiple directions

come against him as he has become a high-value target in the enemy's scope. During this all-out assault, the commander of the universe, who holds all power and might in the palm of his hand, launches a quick reaction force to save one soul. From that moment on, Chad Robichaux becomes one of God's elite Spartans and dedicates his life and soul in the war against spiritual tyranny. Today, Chad and his Spartan wife Kathy have become an unstoppable force for good as they serve, helping to liberate the oppressed with the message of freedom. *An Unfair Advantage* is an intense spiritual fight, good against evil. It's a riveting message that gives anyone who is broken or hurting a sense of hope. It's a must-read!

F. Damon Friedman, PhD
USAF Special Tactics Officer (Combat Controller); Lieutenant Colonel; Iraq and Afghanistan Veteran; 3× Bronze Star Recipient (one for combat valor); Founder & President, SOF Missions; Executive Producer, *Surrender Only To One*

Warriors more than anyone need to understand the spiritual implications of their chosen trade. God has cherished those he has sent into battle from the beginning, and Chad explains how Jesus is the greatest warrior of them all. Take these lessons in spiritual resilience from a true warrior and apply them to your life.

Matthew Heidt, EMBA
US Navy SEAL Senior Chief (Ret.); Iraq Veteran; Bronze Star Recipient for Combat Valor

Chad Robichaux puts the mindset of a true martial artist in his approach to life's many challenges with great success. It is an honor to know his stories of battle in war, competition, and life. And a pleasure to have him as a friend.

Carlson Gracie Jr., "The Prince of Jiu-Jitsu"
Original Gracie Family Member; Head of Carlson Gracie Association

It is incredibly rare to find a book that challenges the human soul with real-life stories that will make your heart race, and break, on almost every page. This is one of those books! A must-read, and perfect gift, for anyone who is struggling with the big questions of life and who is tired of hearing the same old clichés to try to explain them away.

Chris Brown
Senior Pastor, North Coast Church, Vista, California

An Unfair Advantage is truly transformational and is a must-read for every man. Chad has a way of weaving his own story of success and failure together in such a captivating way that you will have a hard time putting this book down. Every competitor I know is always looking for the "advantage," and Chad adds a twist to it in a way that you will never forget. We all talk about the X factor, but few can objectively tell us what it actually is. Chad not only tells us what it is and how to get it, but he also illustrates it from one of the most fascinating life stories you will ever read. What makes Chad so unique is his brutal honesty and humility; he never pulls a punch! It is refreshing to meet a "man's man" who is so secure in his masculinity that he doesn't try to hide or excuse anything. As a pastor and father, I wholeheartedly recommend this book to you!

Tom Ferrell
Lead Pastor of Atascadero Bible Church

AN UNFAIR
ADVANTAGE

VICTORY IN
THE MIDST
OF BATTLE

CHAD M. ROBICHAUX
FOREWORD BY LT. GENERAL "JERRY" BOYKIN

BroadStreet
PUBLISHING

BroadStreet Publishing Group®, LLC
Savage, Minnesota USA
www.broadstreetpublishing.com

AN UNFAIR ADVANTAGE: Victory in the Midst of Battle
Copyright © 2020 Chad M. Robichaux

978-1-4245-6176-6 (paperback)
978-1-4245-6175-9 (hardcover)
978-1-4245-6177-3 (e-book)

All Scripture quotations are taken from The Holy Bible, New International Version® NIV® Copyright © 1973, 1978, 1984, 2011 by Biblica, Inc.™ Used by permission. All rights reserved worldwide. Scripture quotations marked NKJV are taken from the New King James Version®. Copyright © 1982 by Thomas Nelson. Used by permission. All rights reserved. Scripture quotations marked ESV are taken from the ESV® Bible (The Holy Bible, English Standard Version®). Copyright © 2001 by Crossway, a publishing ministry of Good News Publishers. Used by permission. All rights reserved.

Stock or custom editions of BroadStreet Publishing titles may be purchased in bulk for educational, business, ministry, fundraising, or sales promotional use. For information, please email orders@broadstreetpublishing.com.

Cover and interior by Garborg Design at GarborgDesign.com

Printed in the United States of America

20 21 22 23 24 5 4 3 2 1

Then I heard the voice of the Lord saying,

"Whom shall I send? And who will go for us?"

And I said, "Here am I. Send me!"

ISAIAH 6:8 NIV

DEDICATION

From time to time, God causes men to be born, and thou art one
of them, who have a lust to go abroad at the risk of their lives
and discover news. Today it may be of far-off things; tomorrow of
some hidden mountain; and the next day of some near-by men
who have done a foolishness against the State. These souls are
very few; and of these few, not more than ten are of the best.

RUDYARD KIPLING

I wrote this book to challenge and inspire all men to rise up
and be the warriors God created us to be. It is based on
my own experiences as a warrior, and it is dedicated to
each and every brave member of the United States military who
has donned the uniform since 1775, defending the freedoms that
allow me to write these things.

Nothing is more powerful on the battlefield than a man
empowered by the confidence that comes from the knowledge
that he is not fighting alone but acting within the will of God. Such
men have stood boldly in the face of certain death and overcome
extreme odds and adversity—never because it was easy but
because it was right. These are the men who will have extra help

and extra internal resources over their enemy or any personal struggles they may face. They will have an advantage over their opponent that is so great—so lopsided—that it almost seems like an unfair advantage.

I pray this book lights a fire deep within all men and all warriors, past and present, who read it. May they choose to boldly step forward into the battles ahead, fully equipped with the capability to confront and conquer all things.

CONTENTS

FOREWORD

BY LIEUTENANT GENERAL "JERRY" BOYKIN

U ncle Eldon was always different from the rest of the Boykin men when I was growing up in rural North Carolina.
As a youngster, I was always conscious of the fact that
Eldon drank constantly, never seemed to have a job, and spoke
frequently of things that made no sense to me or my cousins who
were my age. Eldon often mentioned his visits to the Veterans
Administration hospital in Durham, North Carolina, where they
never seemed to be able to help him with his issues. He often
came home from a hospital visit with more drugs to help him
sleep, but nothing they gave him seemed to change his behavior,
which was often characterized by a distant stare at nothing in

particular. He frequently spoke of the "ones who died" but without context or a clear reference to exactly of whom he was speaking.

I was keenly aware that "Uncle" Eldon was actually my second cousin and was about my dad's age. I assumed that Eldon was simply different and that maybe the alcohol made him talk and act strangely. Finally, one day my grandmother casually mentioned that Eldon had been at Pearl Harbor when it was attacked. That grabbed my interest because I knew a little about the Japanese attack on December 7, 1941, but I was not well versed on what had actually occurred on that "date which will live in infamy." So, I did two things that helped me understand my uncle better: I studied the attack on Pearl Harbor, and I questioned my dad about what Eldon had experienced. The first task was easy as there were plenty of references available for my study. But when I asked Dad about what had happened to Eldon at Pearl Harbor, he was reluctant to discuss Eldon's experience. It was as if this was a family secret that no one was eager to discuss, almost as if there was something shameful about what had occurred during Eldon's time in the US Army of the Pacific. Confused, I sought out other family members who might be willing to give me the information I was seeking. Eventually, my dad's oldest sister sat down with me and explained what had happened to Eldon on that Sunday morning in the Pacific when the Japanese attacked the US bases in Hawaii, thus bringing America into World War II.

My Aunt Elizabeth was a registered nurse and a woman of considerable patience and great wisdom. She saw that my curiosity was sincere, and she judged that, as a young teenager, I was at an appropriate age to understand the story she would tell me. She explained that on the morning of December 7, Eldon was a young sergeant tasked as "Charge of Quarters" (CQ) for his company at Hickman Field, where US Army Air Corps airplanes were

stationed. As the CQ, Eldon was responsible for alerting his fellow soldiers of any impending danger. The Japanese attack came so quickly and without warning that Eldon was first alerted when Japanese bombs began to fall on the airfield. He ran out of the company headquarters just as enemy bombs exploded along "Battleship Row" adjacent to Ford Island. Confused and desperate to do something to save the men in his company, Eldon ran toward the barracks where the men would be sleeping and relaxing on this Sunday morning. Before he could get to the men, many of them began to pour out of the barracks to see what was happening. As they did, Japanese airplanes strafed the company area, killing and wounding some of the men for whom Eldon felt responsible. He was devastated. Although he continued to run throughout the company area trying to get every man to his assigned battle station, it was too late; the Japanese attack was having a devastating impact on the men and aircraft at Hickman.

Eldon stayed in the US Army at Pearl Harbor until after the war, but he was never the same. He came home in September of 1945 and was soon classified as 100 percent disabled by the Veterans Administration due to "combat stress reaction." I had never heard that term. My aunt explained that it was used to identify people who had experienced horrible things in war that they could not deal with emotionally. She then looked me in the eye and said, "Jerry, they normally call his condition 'shell shocked,' which was first diagnosed during the First World War."

Over the next few years, as I watched Eldon continue to slide into depression and drink himself to an early grave, the question in my mind was why no one could help him. There had to be *someone* who could help him to get beyond what he had experienced at Pearl Harbor and overcome his sense of failure because he could not save every man in his company.

Eldon was just one of tens of thousands of men who came out of the Second World War with the same issues and suffered the same fate. Since then, many who have experienced combat in every war or conflict have dealt with the depression, sleeplessness, and anger that accompanies their memories of combat. Sadly, many stories of these warriors end just as tragically as Eldon's, with a life of alcohol or drug abuse. Some end even worse as many have taken their own lives because of their inability to deal with the emotional stress brought on by their combat experience. Whether it is called "shell shock," "combat stress reaction," "combat fatigue," or "post-traumatic stress disorder" (PTSD)—the most current term—it is a serious problem for many men and women returning from battle, destroying many lives and breaking up many families. The question is whether there is hope for our veterans, or are they simply destined to live depressed, angry, and confused lives?

The US Department of Veterans Affairs has received a great deal of criticism in recent years with incredible stories of veterans having to wait months to get an appointment with a doctor and receive treatment for often life-threatening ailments. While much of this criticism is warranted, it is important to also remember that the number of vets needing care has increased exponentially since the events of September 11, 2001. The VA healthcare system is now treating an unprecedented number of PTSD cases at a time when suicides among vets are at an all-time high. Some estimates range as high as twenty-two vets per day taking their own lives. The burden on the VA system is almost overpowering. One of the consequences of this overload is frequently over-prescribing medications for people diagnosed with PTSD. Medicine certainly may be beneficial in dealing with PTSD, but other things must be more effective and enduring. How do we find those things

that can help our PTSD victims to live better lives free of alcohol, drugs, and medications?

Chad Robichaux is one of those combat warriors who came home from war and struggled with the aftermath of his experiences. His marriage was in serious trouble as were his relationships with others he cared about. Chad was not willing to accept that there was any enemy he could not defeat, especially one so ill-defined as PTSD. But the ultimate victory for Chad was not what he expected.

Chad is the epitome of a warrior. Not only is he a USMC recon non-commissioned officer, but he has also been a police officer and is a well-known competitive mixed martial artist. Chad is a tough guy with all the credentials to prove it. But he finally found an enemy that he could not overcome by just being stronger, faster, and tougher than the adversary. This time he was losing his match, and it was the most important one of his life with everything he cared about at stake. He tried everything he knew, but he was failing. There just *had* to be more. And there was. *Submission* was the answer, but that is not a word that a cage fighter ever uses, unheard of, no way. How could that be the answer?

The story of Chad's struggle is one that brings hope to everyone who has been down the same path after returning to life after combat. Chad found the answer to PTSD, and today, he and his wife have committed their lives to assisting others along the path to recovery and victory through their Mighty Oaks program. I have spent time with Mighty Oaks, and I can attest to its power and record of success.

I wish that Eldon had found a program like this. Maybe his life would have been very different. You see, Chad struggled mightily until he submitted his future to God—every aspect of his life—and found victory. Getting to that point was not easy, but

he finally became the man God wanted him to be, and now he helps others overcome their struggles as a result of combat. I find his story to be compelling and incredible, and I know that many will be touched and helped by it. Let's get this story out to those who need to hear it, to those who suffer the same challenges that Chad did.

Lieutenant General "Jerry" Boykin
US Army Special Forces (36 yrs., retired)
Founding member of the elite US Army Delta Force
US Deputy Undersecretary of Defense for Intelligence
Executive Vice President of Family Research Council
Author, *The Warrior Soul*, *The Coalition*, *Never Surrender*, *Danger Close*
www.KingdomWarriors.net

INTRODUCTION

But we also glory in our sufferings,
because we know that suffering produces perseverance;
perseverance, character;
and character, hope.

Romans 5:3–4

Despite the many ups and downs, I have been blessed to live an amazing life thus far. I am a husband and a father of three incredible children. I am a lifelong martial artist and grappler, having competed at the highest levels, including as a top world ranked[1] pro MMA world champion with an 18-2 pro record,[2] and appearing in the sport's biggest events, such as NBC's *World Series of Fighting*, *StrikeForce*, *Bellator FC*, and *Legacy FC*. I am also an accomplished international Brazilian jiu-jitsu competitor and third-degree Carlson Gracie Jr. black belt. Serving as a law enforcement officer, both locally and federally, I have received a Medal of Valor[3] for bravery beyond the call of duty.

But one of the proudest legacies of the Robichaux family is that we are a three-generation Marine Corps family of combat veterans. My father served as a marine infantry rifleman. I served as

a force reconnaissance marine and DoD contractor (Department of Defense), and my oldest son is now serving as an ANGLICO marine (Air Naval Gunfire Liaison Company). I have had the privilege to serve my country in many ways and places, including eight deployments to Afghanistan as a member of a joint special operations task force.

I have appeared on many national news outlets, ranging from Fox News to *USA Today*, *The Blaze* to *Christian Post*, and many others. And based on my personal experiences, I am considered a subject matter expert on post-traumatic stress disorder (PTSD), having testified in veterans' courts regarding combat trauma and PTSD, advised some of the nation's highest-ranking military flag officers, and advised the current presidential administration on the best and most-effective solutions for veterans' care. While I *do not* believe PTS"D" is a disorder, I *do* use the term in this book for common reference.

In the pages to follow, I intentionally take caution not to mention names of military commands or identify personnel, operational intent, or TTPs (tactics, techniques, and procedures) in order to respect and preserve national security. But I do mention the type of men I served with, and I share a glimpse into the life of special operation missions abroad because this book is about being a warrior, and I have had the privilege to serve with the greatest of them. Through my experiences, I had the privilege to both witness and participate in many incredible situations. Some of these events built us up; others nearly destroyed us, mentally, physically, and spiritually.

Today I continue to serve alongside warriors of the US military through a nonprofit ministry I lead called Mighty Oaks Foundation, which runs Mighty Oaks Warrior Programs. Our primary goal is to bring military warriors to full healing beyond the hard-

ships of their service by simply aligning them with the lives God created them to live. We also serve in the critical role of preparing our warriors for the battles ahead through combat and spiritual resiliency training programs nationwide.

Part of the process includes looking back at the hardships and experiences of their past and allowing the warriors to come to their own realization that however tragic (or heroic) past events may be, they are not what led them to where they are today. Instead, it's the choices they make every day. When a man can come to that realization and take responsibility for his life and his future, only then can he move forward into being the man and the warrior God designed him to be.

If you are searching to find purpose because you've never felt contented or satisfied, you're not alone. Even the most successful men—those with medals pinned across their chests and a long list of accolades—seek something more. It's a burning need so deep that you can't even put your finger on it. It is the feeling of being out of place for your entire life—the feeling of never being quite the person you were supposed to be.

For me, I tried everything to fill this void; some things I am not proud of, and others I am very proud of. However, neither the failures nor the accolades of my life were ever enough. When I faced intense personal struggles after Afghanistan, no pills, counseling, or sports, like Brazilian jiu-jitsu or mixed martial arts, changed my situation. But when I aligned my life with the life God created me to live, I found hope, healing, and a new purpose. In fact, I found what I believe to be the very purpose God created me for, and that is to share what I learned with other warriors like you.

Some will say, "That sounds too easy!" I'll challenge that rebuttal with a question I once had to answer. In fact, I ask every warrior who allows me the privilege to speak into his life the same

question: "If what you are doing isn't working, then why not try something different?" This book will offer you an insight into what that something different is.

Through the chapters ahead, I will share some of my own experiences, including those in the military, as a member of law enforcement, and as a professional fighter, and the lessons we can all learn from inspirational historic warriors of biblical times.

Regardless of your personal beliefs, I ask you to open your heart and mind and challenge yourself to be the very best man and warrior you can be. It is my prayer for you that you will find an unfair advantage to warfare reserved for those who step into the life God created them to live and thus become the warrior you were born to be.

CHAPTER 1

THE KILLING POOL

Above all else, guard your heart,
for everything you do flows from it.

PROVERBS 4:23

Before leaving for my first trip to Afghanistan, I spent four unexpected days alone in Virginia Beach waiting for a military flight. As is common with such flights, I was getting "pushed to the right," meaning delayed for days and shoved chronologically down the calendar. I was frustrated. My preparations were complete. I had already said goodbye to my family and felt at peace although it felt like someone ripped my heart out of my chest after watching my kids stare at me through the car window as they drove away from seeing me off.

I was ready to go—ready to be with my team members in Afghanistan. I was flying out with operators I didn't know, but they were seasoned warfighters who I admired. Since I didn't know any of them personally and they had their own things to do, I stayed to myself. The four days of waiting seemed incredibly long, but all

the training and buildup was over, and soon I was actually going to be doing my job. In those four days, I spent a great deal of time running to burn off nervous energy (I wasn't really nervous, just eager). As I ran along Virginia Beach each day, I passed a giant statue of Neptune, the Roman god of the sea. That statue was warrior-like, and it served as a somewhat grim reminder of the seriousness of what was ahead for me.

For hours at a time, I sat near that statue and stared across the horizon of the Atlantic Ocean trying to imagine what it would be like once I arrived. I realized that somewhere across that ocean was someone who would try to kill me when given the chance. Despite all my training and life experience, I understood that I was still naive as to what it would be like over there, and that unknown intrigued me.

Departure time finally arrived by way of a C-130. I had been on this aircraft many times before on Military Free Fall (MFF) or High Altitude Low Opening (HALO) jumps. As I walked across the tarmac, the fact struck me that I couldn't remember when I had actually returned to the ground inside of one of those planes. I always jumped out before they landed, and to this day, something about the smell of burning jet fuel makes me feel like jumping.

I walked up the back ramp and into the cargo hold. It was loaded with pallets of equipment, supplies, and a small group of operators—some rugged-looking dudes! Unlike some in the military who leave on an international flight with the look on their faces like they may be marching to their deaths, these guys were cracking jokes and seemed excited about doing exactly what they had trained so hard to do. And it was clear that they had done this a time or two before—this was definitely not their first rodeo.

One of the operators I met earlier that week began handing out Ambien sleeping pills for the ride. He was a monster of

a man—about six and a half feet tall and stout enough to be in the NFL—and, like many of these men, he sported long hair and a giant, thick, blond-haired beard. He looked like a Viking. He started to offer me an Ambien but then stopped and pointed at the giant bag next to me—a bag of cash that I was carrying for our team. (He knew about the bag from a briefing we had both attended.) "Why don't you take two of these and then sleep next to me?" he said.

"Not a chance!" I laughed.

He just smiled and handed me the pill. The teasing made me feel welcome among the men for the long journey ahead. Nothing about flying on a cargo plane for twenty-two hours is fun, but like the rest of the guys, I found my own little spot atop a pile of gear, took my Ambien, and balled up like a cat for a long nap.

After a stop in Germany, we arrived at Bagram Air Base, Afghanistan, in the middle of the night. The other guys disembarked and headed off as if they'd been there a hundred times before, but I had an escort to get me squared away. It would be a few hours until I would meet my team. I walked around the outside of the compound, both excited and curious. I wanted to see Afghanistan, but it was still too dark. The cool, dry desert air gave me a familiar feeling of my time as a young recon marine training in Twentynine Palms, California.

I looked at the stars, finding the Big Dipper and the Lazy W to orientate myself north, something I always like to do at night even when I have a GPS. *Wow!* I thought to myself. *I'm really here in Afghanistan. . .and somewhere out there beyond these HESCO barriers and concertina wire is the actual Taliban.* (HESCO barriers are earth-filled metal cages used to make perimeter walls, and concertina wire is coiled razor wire also used at the perimeter.) This thought fascinated me. A few hours later (before the

sun rose), I was leaving the safety of HESCO barriers behind and joining my team off base.

In my initial days, I spent a fair amount of time praying but not for God to save me from my situation; rather, I prayed that I would do a good job and my family would be safe without me. I probably prayed more ritualistically than from any strong confidence that God would take direct action in my family's lives or my own. It was definitely shallow. And instead of allowing my situation to bring me closer to God, over time I allowed it to separate me from him. It didn't take long for God to become an abstract distant concept rather than someone I could lean on in the trials to come.

I was laser focused on my mission and extremely excited, fueled by a passion to take part in retaliating for the attacks on America on September 11, 2001. Like many military personnel who had not served in combat yet, bravado and naivety filled my mind, viewed through patriotic lenses. At the time, I gave little thought to understanding the impact America has globally.

But a short time later, I had an awakening. The things I witnessed on that day (and the following ones) in Kabul, Afghanistan, would change me forever. It wasn't the combat that changed me but rather witnessing the Afghan people on a personal level. They weren't Taliban. I saw life through their eyes. And even though they had a dark history in their nation, they also had a deep appreciation for America.

A local national named Bashir invited me to his home. Over the next few years, Bashir became a trusted teammate and friend. He had invited me to his home to watch the 2004 presidential election unfold. I thought it was strange that he would care, but since I was personally living like a caveman at the time because of my assignment, the prospect of good food and seeing the American election sounded like a great break.

So, another team member and I went to Bashir's home, and to our surprise, the house was packed with his family. There were wall-to-wall people, tons of food for celebration, and every eye was glued to the television, waiting in suspense for the next update. I thought it was incredible that they cared so much about the election of the president of the United States. I had never seen a group of Americans this focused, and these were Afghans! The atmosphere felt like a big Super Bowl party.

These Afghans' candidate of choice was President George W. Bush, and when the results rolled in, the party erupted with dancing, hugging, laughter, and joy. Their reaction blew me away, and in truth, I shared in their excitement. They based their joy on the knowledge that there would be a continued presence of United States and Allied forces in Afghanistan—US forces that had already freed Kabul and many parts of the country from Taliban rule. They feared that, as president, John Kerry would withdraw forces and allow the Taliban to regain control. I understood their thinking, but it would be days later before I had reason to comprehend the depth of their passion.

Over the following days, I continued to talk to Bashir about how amazed I was that his family cared so much about who the US president would be. Bashir decided the best way to show me why they were so passionate about the election was to take me on a tour of his city. What I was about to witness changed my life and heart forever.

Bashir first took me to a four-story apartment building on the east side of Kabul, just off the Jalalabad Road entry into the city. Bullet holes scarred the concrete walls of the apartment building, and the Taliban regime had ripped out the power lines that had once provided electricity to the complex. Bashir had previously taught English here in secret in the basement of the building. He

told me heartbreaking stories of how the Taliban would come into the building, raiding it like a prison inspection and searching for contraband and violations of their rules and laws. Many of the young girls would be raped, beaten, and sometimes killed for having violated their rules or for no reason at all.

Bashir showed me the stairwell leading to the roof where many girls (including one of his twelve-year-old cousins) had committed suicide by throwing themselves off the fourth story rooftop after Taliban thugs had raped or beaten them. Some jumped to avoid such a fate. As I thought of these young girls, I couldn't imagine a fear so deep that it would cause a person to throw themselves off a four-story building to their death. But then I envisioned terrified workers inside the World Trade Center buildings who chose to jump to their deaths rather than burn alive.

The next place we visited was known locally as the Killing Pool. Bashir parked at the base of Mahrus Hill on the north side of Kabul, and a short hike to the top of the hill had us standing in front of a full-size Olympic swimming pool with regulation diving platforms. The structure seemed weirdly out of place in the third-world architecture of Kabul. The Russians built the pool in the 1980s (after they invaded Afghanistan) so that their divers could practice Olympic diving at high altitude (about fifty-nine hundred feet high in Kabul). But I suspect more killing was done here than diving.

As we approached the pool, I immediately noticed a steel cable hanging off the end of the second 7.5-meter diving platform. Someone had drilled a hole through the concrete platform to secure the cable at one end, and on the dangling end was a hangman's slipknot noose. I could only imagine the decapitation that would occur as the noose snapped around someone's neck after falling some twenty-five feet off the platform and coming to an immediate halt at the end of that cable. Bashir said that he

had witnessed public executions here, including when the Taliban would throw men, women, and even children off the top tower onto the concrete floor of the empty pool far below.

But that wasn't the worst of it. As we climbed down the ladder and into the pool, Bashir didn't need to tell me about further atrocities that took place in the Killing Pool. I saw what they were. The deep end of the pool, from sidewall to sidewall—a width of twenty-five meters, or seventy-five feet—was riddled with 7.62-caliber bullet holes from the AK-47 assault rifles commonly used by the Taliban. All the holes were at the elevation of the head of someone who was kneeling. Thousands of holes pierced the walls. And on the shallow end of the pool, at an elevation that would reflect the height of a child, the same bullet pattern riddled the concrete.

I could hardly imagine the horror here not only for those murdered by the Taliban but also those who watched in agony and fear. I took out a Leatherman tool I carried and removed several of the metal jacket remains from the bullet holes—bullets that had certainly killed innocent victims out of the Taliban's hate, greed, lust for power, and desire to be tyrants over the helpless. After that day, I often visited the pool to reflect on what took place there and why I was doing what I did.

Another such reminder was a house where I lived in Kabul. The Taliban, who had converted its basement into a prison, had previously occupied it. Steel hooks hung in the ceiling where they apparently hanged their victims as they tortured them. I would do workouts in the basement and stew over what had likely taken place down there. I bore witness to pain and suffering that no human should ever face.

In truth, the revelations of those days changed me for both the better and the worse. For the remainder of my time in Afghanistan, I wasn't just a patriot retaliating for the treacherous 9/11 attacks

on America, but I was also fueled with the same hatred toward the Taliban that Bashir, his family, and much of the Afghan people held. What I saw took me down a dark path that many military members face after experiencing the atrocities of war firsthand. My heart hardened.

But as I came to know the Afghan people's struggles, my heart also broke with compassion for them—a helpless people who truly experienced oppression at the most grotesque level with no ability to defend themselves. And perhaps most important, I discovered that America does make a difference in this world and that our role matters to others. Regardless of people's political positions and whether or not they thought we belonged in Afghanistan, I know that if even one little girl didn't have to throw herself off the roof of that apartment complex to escape rape and torture, then my time there was worth it. And if just one family didn't have to watch their mother be thrown like a bag of garbage off the ten-meter tower onto the concrete floor of an empty pool below, it was worth it. And if just one less child had to bravely kneel at the shallow end of the Killing Pool and see a monster with an AK-47 assault rifle, it was worth it. Even after all I know now, I'd go back again in a heartbeat, and most of my brothers would do the same.

Seeing the Killing Pool changed the way I saw the world. I pray no person ever experiences such a tragedy as those that occurred at that pool, but I know the world faces similar tragedies every day. We won't end them all, but if we can for one, two, or maybe millions, we must. What would you be willing to do if the Killing Pool was in your neighborhood?

The harsh reality is that when the military goes to war, any war, we pay a price for the sake of others. There will always be a high price paid not only in lives lost but also in the physical, mental, and spiritual aftermath of the warriors who survive. Yet we do

not have to lose our hearts and souls, nor do we have to harden our hearts toward those who have not experienced what we have.

I remember phone calls from my wife when she would tell me she was praying for me, but I often replied that God wasn't in Afghanistan—not in such an evil place. I know now that what I felt wasn't the absence of God but rather the tangible presence of evil. Nonetheless, I allowed hate to fill my heart, and while in Afghanistan, I made a decision that I could not be a Christian. I had developed a faulty belief that Christian men were weak and that I couldn't be a man of morality and a warrior at the same time. I know now that's not true; it's a lie. No one on earth is stronger and tougher than a true man of God, and no one is more equipped to transcend the cruelty and hardship of this world than a man who has God in his heart. But I didn't know this then; by deliberately making a choice to put God on a shelf, it created a hole in my heart that I allowed to fill with hate, rage, and bitterness, and it almost cost me everything.

Many warriors who go to combat face the same moral dilemma. Some completely reject God; others say, "I'll have time for God when I'm older." But it doesn't matter how tough you think you are. You can't successfully engage in a life-or-death conflict when there's a void in your soul. You will fill it with something. Some warriors fill this void with hate, and some even take it to the extreme by adopting war-culture ideologies, acting out as if they were Vikings, Native Americans, or even Nazi death squads. I deeply believe a void created by a lack of spiritual strength causes such actions.

However, there is a definite need for fierce warriors—for those willing to use force against evil aggressors. There is an old quote sometimes attributed to the English novelist George Orwell that says, "People sleep peaceably in their beds at night only

because rough men stand ready to do violence on their behalf." There is a need for warriors who will be violent in the face of evil, but when we exercise that violence, there is a thin line for warriors between doing what is right and doing what is wrong, and deep consequences come with the latter.

There is no need to search for substitutes to living as a man of God—to be the warrior God created you to be. Being a Christian does not mean being weak or that you must relinquish the mantle of being a formidable warrior. Quite the opposite, God calls us to be bold and to stand and fight against evil. The Bible says, "From the days of John the Baptist until now, the kingdom of heaven has been subjected to violence, and violent people have been raiding it" (Matthew 11:12). The Bible is filled with examples of strong men who did violent acts in war without losing their souls, minds, or emotions in that violence. These men didn't have to find a substitute for God; rather, they stood as men of God in the very face of evil.

In reality, an attempt to replace our God-created identity with something else will fail. It's only a matter of time before the false warrior façades we built come crashing down around us, and oftentimes while living out these false identities, we feel trapped by our circumstances. But fortunately, it is a prison with an unlocked door; you can leave it if you wish. On the other side of the door are freedom and the life God intended you to live.

Do you know how circus trainers keep a twelve-foot tall, five-ton elephant from escaping? They put a tiny band around its ankle and tie it to a small wooden stake hammered into the ground, yet an elephant is one of the most powerful animals roaming the earth. In the wild, they regularly push down giant trees, completely uprooting them. As a circus animal, the elephant could take a sin-

gle step to freedom at any moment, and the stake wouldn't stand any more of a chance than a feather in a hurricane.

Why doesn't the elephant just walk away? Because from the moment it was born, trainers taught it to believe a false narrative, and at some point in its life, the elephant believed a lie and lost sight of what it was born to be. These elephants live out their lives in a world they were not created to live within, living as something they were not intended to be, thus missing out on the very nature of what they are and their full potential. They live one step away from freedom; they live in a prison with an unlocked door.

God recognizes that a world infected with wickedness and evil requires warriors to fight and kill tyrants and oppressors in order to preserve freedom, defend the weak, and free the oppressed. The Bible challenges us to "speak up for those who cannot speak for themselves, for the rights of all who are destitute. Speak up and judge fairly; defend the rights of the poor and needy" (Proverbs 31:8–9).

When a warrior aligns his heart with God's purpose, he is more cognizant of and sensitive to exactly what his unlimited duties are in combat. When warrior traditions lack this critical element, it results in otherwise well-intended warriors engaging in the same kind of brutality and savagery that are hallmarks of the Islamic mujahideen. There are surely spiritual consequences to becoming the enemy that you are fighting. Allowing hatred and fear to fuel you will lead to guilt, shame, and bitterness, but fighting with a pure heart results in a victorious spirit. This is not to say that it is unnatural or wrong to hate an evil enemy, but to submit to that hatred and act on its behalf becomes a recipe for disaster. God needs warriors to stand strong in the face of evil and act as a bulwark to defend what is right. If this is your calling, then you do not need to

convince yourself that you are a reincarnated Viking in order to be a berserker on the battlefield and earn a place in Valhalla.

When warriors buy into the lie that we must allow fear, hate, rage, and vengeance to fuel and drive us, we submit ourselves to a false imprisonment and become someone God did not intend us to be. We miss out on the very nature of who we are and the full potential of what it is to be the warrior God created us to be. God has provided spiritual armor for every warrior (see Ephesians 6:10–18), and when we walk boldly onto the battlefield wearing the entire spiritual armor of God under our military armor, it gives us an unfair advantage. For we have the sure knowledge that no matter what fate befalls us, our eternal destiny is secure, so we can fight as true warriors, finding victory in the midst of battle.

CHAPTER 2

GETTING OFF THE X

Some trust in chariots and some in horses,
but we trust in the name of the LORD our God.

PSALM 20:7

y 2004, the Taliban was largely pushed out of the Afghanistan capital city of Kabul, and US forces, International Security Assistance Force (ISAF), and the Afghan National Army (ANA) controlled the inner city. When such times of partial victory and transition of control occur in war-zone strongholds, a premature sense of security begins to develop within local nationals and civilian non-government organizations (NGOs). Sadly, even military personnel sometimes experience a rise in complacency. This makes the good guys a soft target and provides a prime opportunity for terrorist organizations like the Taliban to exploit, which they often did.

During this time, vehicle-borne improvised explosive device (VBIED) attacks, suicide bombings, assassinations, and kidnappings commonly took place inside the Kabul city limits. Because of these sporadic surprise attacks, anyone in the vicinity of the

capital city who looked like the Taliban always caught my attention and kicked my Spider-Man senses into full gear.

Late one afternoon, a teammate and I were driving into the eastern side of Kabul on Jalalabad Road when a Toyota Hilux pickup truck following closely behind me triggered my "spider" senses. Really, the occupants caught my attention. There is a joke we used to tell: "How many Taliban can you fit in a Hilux?" The punch line: "One more!" These guys were piled in the cab and the open bed. They looked pretty dirty, as if they just came out of the mountains, with long beards and tribal garb. The AK-47 assault rifles and what appeared to be a rocket-propelled grenade (RPG) were definite signs that these guys did not belong in Kabul and were up to no good.

My initial thought was that this had nothing to do with us. Dressed in civilian clothes and driving a civilian Toyota Prado (similar to the US model 4Runner), we looked and acted as civilians and were by no means an obvious military target. I drove while my teammate was the only passenger, and both of us were armed only with concealed pistols. We were in no position to get into a gunfight with a Hilux load of Taliban fighters.

Luckily for me, I had just been to our annual driving training at Bill Scott Raceway in Virginia. I always enjoyed learning counter-pursuit driving in high-speed chases, evasive maneuvers, pitting, and ramming techniques—these are a blast to practice, but you never imagine you'll actually use one of them. Something I learned from years of surveillance detection routes training that immediately became useful was to deviate from my route in order to ensure no one was following me.

I turned off of Jalalabad Road; sure enough the Hilux followed. I made a full block and then turned back west on Jalalabad Road; the Hilux was still in tow. This was not good news. The

deviation technique had confirmed they were indeed following us. But it also let them know that we knew they were following us, so they amped up the pursuit and pressed on us even closer.

I made the decision that if I went into the city, I'd stand a better chance of losing them. I was confident in my knowledge of the city, so I fled into the clutter of traffic, but it was nearly a fatal mistake. Like most third-world countries, Kabul traffic can be insane. Rush hour in Los Angeles is nothing compared to this!

I reached a prominent intersection called Massoud Circle (a landmark dedicated to Ahmad Shah Massoud, a national hero of Afghanistan), but the traffic jammed up and the Hilux and its armed occupants somehow pulled about fifteen yards in front of us and stopped, blocking our way forward. They started to pile out the back of the Hilux, and I vividly remember the man who exited the front passenger door of the truck with his AK and how he locked eyes with me.

In my training, we call this being "stuck on the X." The "X" is an ambush point or kill zone. I was now on it. Among the skills you learn in training is to first recognize that you are on the X and, second, that you have to get off it. Simple Marine Corps logic: you can't stay there, or something bad is going to happen. I know if we had stayed on the X that day we could have put up a heck of a fight, but the Taliban would have likely taken or killed us.

One thing I love about the military is its training. For every scenario, you train over and over to the point of redundancy, so when the day for action comes, you don't have to decide what to do; you just do it. At driving training school, we had been through this scenario a dozen times: we solve a roadblock like the one in front of us by a ramming technique. So I floored the gas and aimed my vehicle directly at theirs, and the passenger turned and ran.

When I crashed into the Hilux, I hit it perfectly, and their vehicle

spun out of our way. From the corner of my eye, I got the satisfaction of seeing a few airborne booger-eaters as they flew through the air out the back of the truck. (The term *booger-eater* was my favorite derogatory reference to the Taliban cavemen of Afghanistan.)

After smashing a clear path off the X, we still faced another obstacle. What appeared to be a one-hundred-year-old policeman in his sharp blue uniform gave me an aggressive hand gesture to stop, and he was frantically blowing his traffic whistle at me. I had already hit one person, so being on a roll, I revved my engine and aimed my Prado toward him. The officer, in typical Afghan fashion, quickly jumped aboard the winning team and waved me out of harm's way, even stopping other cars for me to clear the scene.

To this day, I don't know what the true intent was for that attack on us at Massoud Circle. I have my suspicions, but the truth is that if we had stopped on the X that day, I likely wouldn't be writing this book. What kept me moving forward was proper training and a belief that following that training would lead to victory. Having faith in something, and believing in advance that it will result in victory, will always give you the ability to press forward in times when all seems hopeless—when you find yourself on the X.

I wish I could say that I always did this, but at many times in my life, I didn't press forward when I should have. In fact, only a few years later I was diagnosed with PTSD and came home, completely lost, shamed, scared, and hopeless. I was on the X again, but this time, I didn't follow the simple rules. First, I didn't recognize that I was on the X, and second, I didn't take the necessary steps to get off of it. In life, as well as in combat, if we choose to stay on the X, it will lead to our own demise, literally or metaphorically.

The reality is that the same confidence and faith I had in my training that day in Kabul is available to all of us in our everyday lives if we trust God. "'For I know the plans I have for you,'

declares the LORD, 'plans to prosper you and not to harm you, plans to give you hope and a future'" (Jeremiah 29:11). This verse is a promise offered by God to each of us so that when the day of adversity comes and we find ourselves on the X, we can feel assured that moving forward will lead to victory. This promise will never exempt us from the hardships of this world, but those who trust this promise and pursue a life within God's will can be assured that on the other side of hardships we will find ourselves where we were meant to be.

In the Bible, in the book of Exodus, we see the same promise given to the Israelite people: a promise of prosperity, hope, and a future. To deliver that promise, God called Moses to stand up against all of Egypt—including the Pharaoh, the mighty ruler of Egypt—in order to set his people free and lead them into the promised land.

The Israelite people had been captive for hundreds of years, living a life of bondage, slavery, and poverty in Egypt. Moses spread word to the Israelites that they would be free men in the days ahead and live a life of prosperity in the promised land. I can imagine the singing, dancing, and celebration that must have taken place. But just as in military training, promises of good times must be tested and proven under pressure. Sure enough, the Israelite people soon found themselves on the X and in the line of fire of Pharaoh and his minions.

Pharaoh initially agreed to let the Israelites go free, but as Moses prepared to lead them out of Egypt, Pharaoh changed his mind. Following a series of ten massive miracles (often called the ten plagues), Pharaoh let them go. When Moses and the newly freed Israelites reached the Red Sea, they camped there. But God allowed Pharaoh's heart to harden, which caused him to change his mind once again, and he decided to go after them

and kill them—not with a Hilux truck full of Taliban but with the entire Egyptian army. Every horse and chariot in the army closed in around Moses and the unarmed Israelite people, who had long been Egyptian slaves. On the banks of the Red Sea, the Israelites found themselves stuck on the X, and instead of getting off it, they stayed there and fell apart.

Exodus 14:10 tells us: "As Pharaoh approached, the Israelites looked up, and there were the Egyptians, marching after them. They were terrified and cried out to the Lord." Why is it that we only start praying when things go wrong, even when God has already given us his promise as to the outcome?

And as most people do when things fall apart, the Israelites looked for someone to blame. "They said to Moses, 'Was it because there were no graves in Egypt that you brought us to the desert to die? What have you done to us by bringing us out of Egypt? Didn't we say to you in Egypt, "Leave us alone; let us serve the Egyptians"? It would have been better for us to serve the Egyptians than to die in the desert'" (vv. 11–12). They lacked faith in God's promises and announced they'd rather go back to the known way of being slaves than the new way of being free.

How many times do we find ourselves in this position of choosing the known and bad over the unknown and new? We initially move toward the freedoms found in the promises of God, but when the going gets tough, we somehow prefer to go right back to the bondage.

In the chaos of being stuck against a sea with no exit route in the face of the advancing Egyptian army, Moses calmed the people and reminded them of the victory promised by God. Moses said, "Do not be afraid! Stand firm and you will see the deliverance the Lord will bring you today. The Egyptians you see today

you will never see again. The Lord will fight for you; you need only to be still" (vv. 13–14).

"Then the LORD said to Moses, 'Why are you crying out to Me?'" In other words, "Why are you praying right now? I already made a promise to you! Act on it!" God then said, "Tell the Israelites to *move on*" (v. 15). In short, get off the X!

Many of us probably know the rest of the story: Moses split the Red Sea and the Israelites walked through on dry ground with a wall of water on their right and on their left. They were on their way off the X. Pharaoh and the Egyptian army, to their own demise, decided to chase them, but "the water flowed back and covered the chariots and horsemen—the entire army of Pharaoh that had followed the Israelites into the sea. Not one of them survived" (v. 28).

There are many parallels between my moment on Massoud Circle and Moses' moment on the banks of the Red Sea. We will all find ourselves on the X at some point, whether in combat or in life. The question is what will we do when we are there. Will we choose to stay on the X only to get dragged back to where we came from? Will we stay there and die? In Kabul, I recognized the situation and pressed forward; Moses, when he found himself on the X, was strong in his faith, believed in God's promised victory, and led the others forward.

"'For I know the plans I have for you,' declares the LORD, 'plans to prosper you and not to harm you, plans to give you hope and a future'" (Jeremiah 29:11). This is a promise to you, me, and everyone willing to accept it, regardless of your situation. When the day of adversity comes (and it will) and you find yourself on the X (and you will), you can be assured that moving forward with a firm reliance on God will result in victory. This is an unfair advantage available to each of us, whether on the battlefield or in everyday life.

CHAPTER 3

VALLEY OF THE SHADOW OF DEATH

Even though I walk through the darkest valley
(the valley of the shadow of death),
I will fear no evil, for you are with me;
your rod and your staff, they comfort me.
You prepare a table before me in the presence of my enemies.

PSALM 23:4–5

I sat in the backseat of my Land Rover Defender next to my Pakistani friend Shahr. We both had taken a break from conversation, so there was a quiet moment on our twenty-plus hour trip into the mountainous region of the Federally Administered Tribal Area (FATA). The tribal region was a blurred borderline between the countries of Afghanistan and Pakistan.

I focused my gaze out of the passenger side window and enjoyed the surprising peace I found in the beauty of the landscape. I often enjoyed traveling through the mountains there as the

region offered some of the most beautiful and spectacular scenery I'd seen anywhere. In this part of the world where the Karakoram, Himalayan, and Hindu Kush mountains meet (the three largest mountain ranges on the planet), it creates a landscape that makes America's Rocky Mountains look like a Kansas hillside. I can best describe it as a scene from *The Lord of the Rings* films, with endless peaks and valleys ranging from two thousand feet above sea level to more than twenty thousand feet.

But the landscape's majestic beauty can be deceiving, for it is brutal not only with deadly weather and treacherous terrain but also with the evil that lurks throughout the area. It is a safe haven for Taliban warfighters moving in and out of the FATA to fight US and NATO forces, so my mind did not remain content or complacent for long. There was risk and danger at every step on this trip. We were definitely in Indian country and a place where I didn't belong, but the importance of the work we were doing was more than enough motivation to outweigh the risk.

My mission was to conduct a feasibility study of a specific remote area that my task force was targeting for operations. Neither Natiq (our driver) nor Shahr knew the real reason for our trip. As part of my job, I had lied to them about my intentions for traveling to this area, and we had no weapons to defend ourselves and no military backup or quick response force (QRF) to bail us out.

Natiq, a nineteen-year-old city boy who was still a kid, was likely the most uncomfortable of the three of us. Shahr, who was much older than me, had grown up in the mountains of Pakistan and spent most of his life as a Sherpa (someone who essentially serves as a human pack mule for high-mountain expeditions). He eventually became a skilled mountain guide on such summit expeditions as K2 and Nanga Parbat, two of the highest and most dangerous mountains on earth. (K2, known as the "Savage

Mountain," is located in Pakistan and is the world's second-highest mountain. Nanga Parbat, called the "Killer Mountain," is the western anchor of the Himalayas.)

Shahr, who knew the region well, was able to get the necessary permits for access and had lined up lodging for our travels in safe Ismailia villages where he had personal family connections. All Ismailia Muslim people, a sect of the Shia Muslims known to be much friendlier to foreigners, had vowed to protect any guests they hosted. During my travels, I gained a great deal of respect and love for these people, and I always appreciated their warm hospitality.

Our drive deeper into the mountains gradually changed from uninhabited terrain to an inhabited tribal area, so my eyes shifted focus from the distant horizons to the nearby human environment that posed the greatest threat to my personal safety. I found it fascinating that the farther into the wilderness we traveled, the more extreme the Muslim culture became. Women above the age of eleven or twelve years old were nowhere in sight. The men stared with deep hatred toward most westerners, reminding me once again that I wasn't in the land of Mom and apple pie.

This was the land the American public didn't understand—a place where the underlying lifeblood of the culture was rooted in jihadi violence and inner cultural rivalry designed to control all others through intimidation and fear. It wasn't that they had chosen this form of society over another; it's that they had never known any other, possibly for centuries. This was one of those moments where the comfort of knowing about Shahr's connections kept me moving forward.

Somehow the people here managed to staple a village to the side of a hill steep enough to be a difficult climb. How anyone ever thought that building homes in terrain like that was a good idea

was beyond me, but it was a spectacular sight and common to this part of the world. As we drove through the village, the local populous was dense with rough and rugged men who looked like jihadist radicals who might be having a day off from fighting. I noticed that Shahr and Natiq remained eerily quiet. It wasn't until we had cleared the village that either of them allowed himself to breathe.

Shahr offered, "I didn't want to say anything, Mr. Chad, in fear that you would not want to keep going. But all of those men back there were Taliban. If we stopped, they would probably have killed us all."

Shahr and I both noticed that Natiq was barely breathing and scared to death. I'm not sure why, but Shahr and I both broke out laughing, probably at Natiq's fear but also out of relief. Natiq's continued silence made the humor even more enjoyable.

But maybe five hundred yards out of the village, our laughter came to an immediate halt. A rockslide from the steep mountains had buried the road, and a long line of stopped vehicles built up in front of us. With the mountain range on one side and a steep whitewater river valley on the other, we had no way around the slide. We were now trapped near the very village that moments before we had been morosely joking about being murdered in. I immediately did a mental inventory of what I had on me: an iridium satellite phone, a backpack with supplies for three weeks, and climbing axes.

Without warning, Shahr immediately jumped out of the vehicle and ran up and over the rockslide. The moment he disappeared out of sight, the mountainside gave way even more, tripling the size of the blockage. I didn't often find myself at a loss for what to do, but the situation truly caught me by surprise. I tried to convince myself that Shahr was not buried beneath the mountainside and that I was not stuck there alone in the middle of

Indian country, which certainly seemed the reality at that moment. I did my best to remain calm and assess the problem, but our new Land Rover had unfortunately become the center of attention for the people of the village. Boys of nearly all ages were staring and speaking about it, just as they would in America. I may not have fully understood the language, but boys are boys regardless of where they are in the world when it comes to fancy new vehicles.

Things could go south in a place like this very quickly, so I decided the best thing for me to do was to grab my backpack, axes, and the sat phone and get a better look at the rockslide. If I needed to beat feet out of there, it was better to get away from the car and have my gear with me. Natiq, looking pretty scared, stayed at the vehicle, dumbfounded at the whole situation.

I tried to use the sat phone, but with the thick snow clouds overhead, it couldn't find a good signal. My attempt to contact a member of my team back in the rear had failed. (With America's involvement in remote places of the globe, it is my hope that there will soon be some serious advance in military communication ability. But I imagine that this has been the same wish of nearly every warrior on the battlefield throughout all time, for communication technology is never good enough, and it always fails at the worst possible time.)

An hour later, with tensions among travelers and villagers mounting and my own blood pressure rising even faster, I witnessed an incredible sight: Shahr walking back over the rockslide.

"Mr. Chad! Come! I have a ride for us!"

Shahr ran back to the vehicle, grabbed his bag, and told Natiq to take the Land Rover and meet us at our final destination whenever he could get there. Here was a city boy, stuck out in bad-guy territory and scared to death, who just heard that he was

on his own with a fifty-thousand-dollar vehicle. Poor Natiq! I felt bad for him but knew we needed to press on.

As we headed over the rockslide, I grew increasingly nervous about the rocks giving way under our feet. And then I looked behind me and saw a bizarre sight. At least a hundred other travelers had taken our cue and were following our lead. Whole families, some carrying suitcases on their heads, had abandoned their vehicles and started hoofing it across the treacherous rockslide without regard for safety.

"Why are they following us?" I asked Shahr.

"They don't want to stay in this area any more than we do," he replied.

Feeling alone as an American and finding myself in such a crazy situation, I had naively thought I was the only one in danger who needed to escape that particular area. But I wasn't alone; they all wanted out and needed someone to go forward. That day it was Shahr, and then I followed, and then the others followed too. In the midst of the chaos and selfishly concerned with getting out of there for our own safety, we unwittingly blazed a trail forward for strangers in need and in the most unexpected of places.

On the other side of the rubble was a Honda Accord with a complete stranger for a driver, who had agreed to take us where we needed to go for sixty dollars. It was going to be several more hours, so I laid down in the back to get some shut-eye. I'm not sure what became of the others who followed us, but I do know they left that village only because we went first.

When you find yourself in an impossible situation, you often think you are alone. It is easy to focus on yourself, your own circumstance, or even your own self-pity and miss the fact that many around you are facing similar challenges. We all need a leader to follow, and sometimes you must be that leader. Someone must go

first, and God loves to use those who are willing to take a first step. It is those steps of faith that can lead us to experience the victory that comes from a life willing to follow God. But how is it done?

One of the best examples I can give is from the Bible regarding the life of Jonathan, the son of King Saul of Israel. An incredible warrior, Jonathan fought bravely on the battlefield throughout his life. He also possessed a steadfast faith in the Lord. First Samuel 14:1–23 tells one of my all-time favorite battle scenes. Jonathan's father (King Saul) and the Israelite army were hiding in caves in the mountains after having lost a battle against their enemy, the Philistines. As the king and the army sat in fear, Jonathan recognized that someone had to go first, so he made a bold decision to start a fight. Without telling his father or anyone else, he asked his armor-bearer to sneak with him into the enemy's camp and bring the fight to the bad guys.

As they began their trek, Jonathan said to his armor-bearer, "Perhaps the LORD will act in our behalf. Nothing can hinder the LORD from saving, whether by many or by few" (v. 6). In the darkness of night, the two warriors climbed up cliffs on hands and feet. As they neared the enemy, Jonathan assured his comrade, "The LORD will act in our behalf!" Jonathan's armor bearer replied, "Do all that you have in mind…I am with you heart and soul" (v. 7). Any man reading this right now, and especially another warfighter, has to be motivated by this bold statement of loyalty, or else you don't have a pulse!

You decide to do something really crazy, and you want an accomplice. You reach out to the brother who you know will go to the gates of hell with you and say, "Hey! No one else is going to fight the enemy. They are over there, and I'm going to sneak into their barracks and start killing bad guys. You in?" We'd all want the same reply Jonathan got from his armor-bearer: "I am with

you heart and soul." Let's get 'em! "Come on, then," Jonathan replied (v. 8).

The two quietly reached the Philistines' camp, entered the enemy barracks, and killed twenty men, creating a panic in their ranks. In the dark, the Philistines didn't know who or how many had attacked them. King Saul heard the panic and did what any military leader would still do today: he took a headcount to see if anyone was missing. He found that Jonathan and his armor-bearer were gone.

Once the king realized the two were gone and he could hear the fighting and the Philistines shouting in panic, Saul said, "Never mind; let's get going!" Then Saul and all his men rushed out to the battle and found the Philistines killing each other. The Israeli army joined the fight; even the Hebrews who had deserted and those who had been hiding joined in conquering the Philistine forces. They won a great battle that day because one man led the way.

When you find yourself in an impossible situation, you may feel scared. Hope may seem lost. You may think you are completely alone, but you are not. Others have that same fear, feel equally hopeless, and think they are alone. Many times I have been in fear of my life (like being nearly trapped in that village), feeling all alone and not sure where to go next. I have no doubt that as Jonathan and his armor-bearer climbed the mountainside to face the impossible odds of slaying the Philistine enemy, they had the same thoughts. But they were not alone. We are never alone. Whether we acknowledge him or not, the Lord is always there.

We all share the same fears, doubts, and struggles. It is always easier for us to focus on ourselves, our own circumstances, or our own self-pity and miss that fact that many around us are facing similar struggles—like those who needed someone to lead them out of that village in the FATA or like King Saul and

the Israelites who needed a brave warrior to start the fight. We all need a leader to follow, but you will need to be that leader at times. Someone must go first.

Neither Shahr nor I walked out of that village in the FATA due to our faith in the Lord, but that wasn't the case with Jonathan. It was not only Jonathan's courage to lead when others wouldn't but also his steadfast and unwavering faith in the Lord that gave him an unfair advantage. He inspired others to follow him into the battle and find victory for the nation of Israel.

CHAPTER 4

THE GIRL ON
CHICKEN STREET

I consider that our present sufferings
are not worth comparing with the glory
that will be revealed in us.

ROMANS 8:18

L ife is a balancing act when you're living off-base and are immersed within the local population in a war zone. If you lean too far toward complacency, you become a soft target, and if you lean too far toward paranoia, you show your cards and become a worthy target. Walking that tightrope is intense. Our hectic operations tempo seemed to consistently work us twenty hours a day, seven days a week. So, with that schedule, we needed a break from the reality of our missions from time to time.

One morning, one of my teammates, Bink, an avid golfer, was reading an issue of *Time* magazine and came across an article on the most dangerous golf courses in the world.[4] As fate

would have it, the number one course was in none other than Kabul, Afghanistan. Since I was in charge, Bink wouldn't let up on me about hitting the pause button and taking a break to test out the golfing "greens" of Kabul. He was right about all of us needing a break, so I agreed, and we set out to see if this golf course was the real thing.

After navigating into the outskirts of the city, sure enough, we found that this place actually existed. But the construction of the greens told the tale of this nine-hole course: they were portable mats of artificial turf that the caddies also used to set up your tee. One of my favorite photos is of me putting on the fifth hole while an armored ISAF convoy was on patrol only one hundred yards behind me. We had a great day and really were overdue for a break from the strain of our daily grind.

While we occasionally tried to make time for moments of fun, for the most part, days like this golf outing in Kabul were far outside the norm. Most often, the highlight of our week was our grocery run to town, but those days were unpredictable because we needed to vary our schedule and times to avoid setting any patterns that would make us a target or allow someone to coordinate a planned attack on us.

Downtown Kabul is an interesting place. The Afghan people seem to live a normal life even during times of war, and they're good at it because they've been doing it for thousands of years. We often liked to visit a street known as Chicken Street. It's an old trading post from British days back in the 1800s. With the foreign NGO personnel present nearby, it became a favorite place for vendors to sell souvenirs, rugs, and all the latest pirated DVDs. Even though the presence of the foreigners made it a security risk, the local Kabul police and the ANA kept it fairly secure. Those authorities did not permit cars on the street because of concerns of a VBIED.

Frankly, however, the biggest threat on Chicken Street was usually the harassment of the local kids selling anything they could to make a buck. We named one of those rough and tough Kabul street kids Bob, and he soon became Bink's regular sidekick. We would hire Bob to take us shopping and keep the other kids away. He could have been a good marine had he grown up in the States. Bob had many traits that people who have spent time with marines would easily recognize, and he immediately responded to orders. "Bob, get rid of that kid harassing us!" And Bob was on it. One fewer nagging kid and the others would scurry off ... for a while at least. That may sound callous, but the sad truth is that Bink, myself, and others had cold, hardened hearts during this time in our lives. But for every ten rough and tough Bobs, one street kid would capture the heart of the toughest warrior, and that's exactly what happened to us.

I never knew her name, but she was always on Chicken Street with her sister, selling maps and newspapers written half in English and half in Dari, the local language of Kabul. She was probably nine years old, and like a few other Afghan girls I'd seen, she had dark olive skin and amazingly beautiful aqua-blue eyes. Something about her and her sister made my heart break as I witnessed the harsh poverty these kids had to live in. To endure the frozen winters without shelter and to experience hunger that verges on starvation are realities most Americans will never witness.

I bought a paper from her, probably paying fifty times the actual value, and she smiled as I went into the store she was peddling in front of. We purchased things off my grocery list, and Bink bought Pepsis for both the girl and her sister. As we exited the store, Bink gave them each a Pepsi, and she smiled again and said, "*Tashakor*," meaning "Thank you." Bink gave his best

attempt in reply: "*Qabele tashakor nest*," or "You are welcome." Shopping was always a good time to practice our Dari.

Bink, Bob, and I had walked a block away from the girls when we heard the concussive sound of an explosion. We looked back to where we had just been and saw dust spreading through the air and people screaming and running away. It was time to go. This was not our fight. Our day of shopping and picking out new DVDs was over. We quickly made it to our car.

Later that day, one of our local team members reconnected with Bob and learned what had happened. A Chechen suicide bomber had a string of hand grenades attached to his body. He had located a few ANA soldiers on a security patrol where we had been and self-detonated to kill them. The soldiers, fortunately, only suffered wounds, and the Chechen terrorist had blown himself to pieces, but the collateral damage was two dead children. One was our little friend with aqua-blue eyes. She was simply trying to raise enough money to survive life on the hard streets that day, but instead, a terrorist murdered her. I could only hope that she was enjoying the Pepsi that Bink had given her and that she had died quickly, being happy for the moment from a sugar rush.

These types of atrocities filled my heart with hate and made me feel like a raging madman at times. Seeing the brutality of the world is not only something that can enrage you, but it can also confuse you. Without an eternal perspective on life and living, it is difficult to observe evil in this world and not ask, "Why do bad things happen to good people?" Or "If there really is a God, why does he allow evil to exist?" Fair questions.

I don't think anyone would believe God willed those two innocent children's deaths on Chicken Street that day. He didn't orchestrate his majestic plan to have a suicide-bomber murder them. But could he have stopped it? That question perplexed me. Could the

God of creation, who hung the galaxies and universe and who is beyond time and space, have protected these precious children from an unnecessary and brutal death? Of course he could! *So, why didn't he?* That question ate at me throughout my life.

As I think of that poor girl on Chicken Street, it's tough to see how it all fits together, but I have seen and experienced enough of God's work in the world to believe that it does fit together. The only plausible answer to my question, *Why didn't he?*, would simply be that we don't have all the answers; we can't see everything that God can. That is what faith is all about. As a man, I want answers, but I've learned that instead I need to create a box in my brain in which to store the "I don't know the answer to this" subject material. Rather than obsess over those questions, I trust God's Word: "As the heavens are higher than the earth, so are my ways higher than your ways and my thoughts than your thoughts" (Isaiah 55:9).

Although we may not fully understand the mysteries of God's eternal plan, the Bible gives us clear examples to strengthen our confidence that he is in control and that his plan for us in the grand scheme is to do us good and not harm. (Remember Jeremiah 29:11: "'For I know the plans I have for you,' declares the LORD, 'plans to prosper you and not to harm you, plans to give you hope and a future.'")

Why do bad things happen to good people? First, none of us is *good*. Jesus was the only One who was truly good, and the rest of us will always fall short on that scale. Still, even Jesus had it tough: he was born in a manger, cribbed in an animal's feeding trough, lived his life on the run, faced false accusations, and then his own people captured, tortured, and murdered him. That's what happened to the good guy! This clearly proves that bad things sometimes happen, and it is not God who does us harm, but rather this broken world remains the culprit.

God could have designed us with the internal programming to always love him and never do anything wrong to ourselves or to others. He could have produced robots, but he didn't. In order to have an authentic relationship with each of us, God gave us a choice in the matter. That he did so proves his love for us, and when we make the right choice in response, it proves our love for him. But having the choice, many will choose not only to reject him but also to commit acts of murder, rape, and even genocide. In a world filled with selfish agendas and choices, consequences will always exist because the bad and sinful actions of others can affect and harm us.

One of my heroes from the Bible is the apostle Paul, who, like each of us, fell far short of perfection. But because of his willingness, and even despite his dark past and sordid experiences, God used him. Before he was the apostle Paul, he was simply Paul, and before that, others knew him as Saul—a religious Pharisee who took up the mantle to destroy Christianity. He persecuted and killed Christians, broke apart people and families, and sought to eliminate anything suggesting that Jesus had risen and was the long-awaited Messiah. If he were alive today, he'd be the modern-day ISIS jihadist, hell-bent on exterminating Christianity and those who profess it.

But Saul's life changed dramatically during a trip to Damascus around 34 AD.[5] He and his band of men had an encounter with the risen-from-the-dead Jesus. A glorious light appeared around them so bright that it literally blinded Saul. It was like looking into the sun from only feet away. He fell to the ground, terrified, and heard a voice speaking to him from within the light. As he reported in Acts 26, "We all fell to the ground, and I heard a voice saying to me in Aramaic, 'Saul, Saul, why do you persecute me? It is hard for you

to kick against the goads.'" Saul replied, "Who are you, Lord?" Then he heard, "I am Jesus, whom you are persecuting" (vv. 14–15).

Saul slowly lifted his head and asked, "Lord, what do you want me to do?" Jesus replied, "Arise and go into the city" (Acts 9:6). So Saul, now blind, was led into the city where he met a man named Ananias, who Jesus had told to give Saul his new mission: Saul was to become a Christian, align himself with those he had been persecuting, and declare the gospel of Jesus to the Gentiles (that is, the non-Jews). On that day, Saul changed his Jewish name and adopted the Gentile name Paul. With his new name and a new mission, Paul worked for the next thirty-two years until the Roman government had him killed as a result of his unwavering faithfulness to his mission.

Paul is a great example of someone who was once evil but was later changed by the grace of God. He, too, had to grapple with the same questions I mentioned earlier. After his conversion, no one on earth was arguably more dedicated to God and did more good than the apostle Paul, yet he experienced more trouble than most of us could ever imagine.

First, for a long time, even though he fully committed himself to the cause of Christ, his fellow Christians did not accept him. After all, he had been killing them. So, when he went to the other apostles and said, "Hey fellas! I'm on your team now," it didn't go over well, and how can we blame them? If I received an application from ISIS leader Abu Bakr al-Baghdadi claiming he had rejected his radical Islam exploits and now wanted to join my team to work with combat vets, I might feel suspicious and would ask more than a few questions, including, "What has changed since last week, when you stuffed Christians into cages and set them on fire?" This was what Paul faced. "All those who heard him

were astonished and asked, 'Isn't he the man who raised havoc in Jerusalem among those who call on this name?'" (Acts 9:21).

Second, his new faith caused him a lot of strife with those who didn't like Christians. As he explained:

> I have worked much harder, been in prison more frequently, been flogged more severely, and been exposed to death again and again. Five times I received…forty lashes minus one. Three times I was beaten with rods, once I was pelted with stones, three times I was shipwrecked, I spent a night and a day in the open sea, I have been constantly on the move. I have been in danger from rivers, in danger from bandits, in danger from my fellow Jews, in danger from Gentiles; in danger in the city, in danger in the country, in danger at sea; and in danger from false believers. I have labored and toiled and have often gone without sleep; I have known hunger and thirst and have often gone without food; I have been cold and naked. Besides everything else, I face daily the pressure of my concern. (2 Corinthians 11:23–28)

He was also bitten by a venomous snake, held in prison in Jerusalem for two years without trial, and faced many other hardships while executing his mission. Yet Paul never let the guilt of his past atrocities or the intense opposition he sometimes faced hold him back from the new mission God had given him.

Even while wrongly imprisoned in the basement of a brutal dungeon, he continued to write powerful messages of optimism and encouragement to other Christians, instructing them how to live out their Christian beliefs. The godless Roman government,

assisted by those who had once been Paul's own people, eventually martyred him for his faith.

Yet through his long life filled with difficulties and suffering (more than most of us could ever bear), we never see Paul asking, *Why, God?* We never see him lose his faith or let his hardships, sufferings, or the evil he repeatedly experienced stop him from his mission. No, he finished his mission and finished it well. As he openly acknowledged, "I have fought the good fight, I have finished the race, I have kept the faith" (2 Timothy 4:7).

Paul worked hard in this evil and broken world to rescue others from it. He knew the purpose for which he was born: to be a warrior for the kingdom and fight the good fight of sharing God's truth with others, which gave him an unfair advantage throughout his life.

CHAPTER 5

CREATED FOR A PURPOSE

The greatest tragedy is not death,
but a life without purpose.

MYLES MUNROE

The Bible makes it abundantly clear that God created man and that he created him for his glory: "Everyone who is called by my name, whom I created for my glory, whom I formed and made" (Isaiah 43:7). Therefore, the ultimate purpose of man, according to the Bible, is simply to glorify God. A harder question to answer, perhaps, is what does it look like to glorify God? We fulfill our purpose of glorifying God by living our lives in relationship and faithful service to him. As a man, in order to glorify God, you will need to be the warrior and leader he made you to be to win your own battles. Whether in Iraq, Afghanistan, or at home, *all* men face the battles of life, and God created us to *win* those battles. But to find victory you must first understand and live out *your* purpose of glorifying him.

I was only seventeen years old when I enlisted in the Marine

Corps. After my rough childhood and dysfunctional family life, the Marine Corps provided a clean slate—a fresh start—and I embraced every aspect of it. I was now on the path to accomplish one of my biggest childhood dreams: becoming a Force Recon marine. I have always considered it one of the greatest honors of my life to be part of the "Brother Recon" community where I have lifelong brothers. The basic reconnaissance course to become a recon marine has one of the highest attrition rates in the Department of Defense, an 80 percent dropout rate. It operated out of Coronado, California, next door to Basic Underwater Demolition School (BUDs) or SEAL training. If you have never been to Coronado and felt the bone-chilling cold of that water, the ocean temperatures in allegedly sunny California stay frigidly cold year-round, and I think God planned it that way to make recon marines and Navy SEALs just a little bit tougher.

I remember the "wetsuit-appreciation days" (which means we *couldn't* use our wetsuits on those days); we would lay in the surf zone with our arms locked and the breaks of the waves crashing down on us. Our instructors did not allow us to even do push-ups or flutter kicks because it would warm us. With our teeth chattering and every muscle tensed from the freezing water, I recall the instructors saying, "We are not leaving till five people quit."

I was there with some of the toughest, most hardheaded Devil Dogs (a nickname given to marines by the Germans in WWI at the Battle of Beleau Wood in France due to their ferocious fighting spirit[6]), but the cold, wet, sandy days have a tendency to break even the toughest of men. I remember thinking that this rite of passage was stupid. It seemed like a "someone did this to me, so I'll do it to you" kind of thing; that wasn't it at all. I now know that it was to show those of us who didn't quit what recon marines are made of so that one day in the future, when you go into a

cave in Afghanistan or charge through a door and into a room full of bad guys, you don't have to look over your shoulder to know if your brothers are behind you. You already know they are because you've seen them persevere in the worst if circumstances. You've seen them break but keep going, even when broken. You learn who you are, and you know who is on your left and right. It's the fires of hardship that forge us into our very best.

Whether in war or everyday life, everyone goes through hardship. But the warrior has an advantage. We've been through struggles and have come out on the other side, which is what it's all about. Persevering in our battles molds us into who we were born to be.

There is a story of a man walking through the forest and seeing a caterpillar's cocoon hanging from a branch. He thought it would be an incredible experience to witness the transformation of life when the cocooned caterpillar emerged as a butterfly and took flight, so he broke off the branch holding the cocoon and brought it home. He hung it over a jar on top of his windowsill and waited and watched. One morning as he was walking by, he saw the cocoon moving and thought, *Today is going to be the day!*, so he took the cocoon and laid it on the table, grabbed a cup of coffee, pulled up a chair, and waited for the big show.

It started to happen. The cocoon started shaking violently, and in a moment there was a small crack on the surface. A fierce struggle began as the butterfly fought to break open the rigid walls of the cocoon and emerge into the world, but it looked like it wouldn't make it out. The butterfly's little feet seemed to be unsuccessful in the struggle to pull open the crack in the cocoon's outer shell. The man grew concerned. Even though the butterfly's head had popped out, it didn't seem as if the butterfly would make it, so the man decided to intervene. He picked up the cocoon and

gently and carefully tore it open with his fingers. As he pulled the walls of the cocoon away from the butterfly's body, the beauty of the butterfly was finally revealed. The butterfly attempted to spread its wings, but then it fell flat on the table and died.

As it turns out, the struggle was necessary for the butterfly to be what God created it to be and do what God created it to do: spread its wings and fly. I've been told that as the butterfly pushes its wings against the cocoon walls, it releases a chemical needed to strengthen the wings for flight. The struggle is part of the process; it's part of the master design. Robbed of the struggle, the butterfly could not live; it never became what it was born to be. Persevere through your struggles.

The Bible teaches us this same lesson. The apostle Paul wrote that we are to boast in our sufferings because we know that "suffering produces perseverance; perseverance, character; and character, hope" (Romans 5:3–4). There is value in struggles, but you may have to wait until you're on the other side to understand how it helped you become who you were born to be.

The struggles of my life started far before I became a marine. I experienced a childhood of physical abuse from a Marine Corps Vietnam veteran father. I also experienced the abandonment of my parents and the profound pain caused by the murder of my teenage brother. I joined the US Marines Corps for a fresh start at life and then began my journey to become a Force Recon marine. It was ten years later before I stepped foot onto a real-life combat zone.

After eight deployments as part of a joint special operations task force, I spent the next three years recovering from PTSD. I never would have thought in a million years that I would suffer from PTSD. My masculine ego convinced me I was above that, yet there I was, in my prime of life, believing I was saving the free world but at the same time facing the greatest enemy

I'd ever faced: myself. The physiological symptoms overtook me, things like numbness in my face and extremities, feeling my airway swelling shut, panic attacks, memory loss, and so forth. I felt like a runaway train looking for a place to crash, and doctors prescribed a strong array of medications.

Due to my security clearances and the nature of the programs I was involved in, the PTSD diagnosis resulted in immediate removal from my job, teammates, and what I believed was my only purpose in life. I felt devastated, ashamed, and lost. I believed I had failed, and in part, I was told that I had. I had put everything into our mission and my occupation as a warrior, and now I found myself lost and hopeless about the future. This state of mind drove me on a self-fulfilling-prophecy agenda that devastated the world around me and those who loved me, nearly costing my family and me everything we had.

Today, I stand on the other side of all those circumstances. I know that the struggles molded me into the man I am today. I have learned great lessons, and I must share them with others who are facing or will face similar struggles so that we can endure them and emerge on the other side as the men God created us to be. This is what we see in the story of Joseph from the Bible. Not Mary's husband but rather the Joseph with the "amazing technicolor dreamcoat" (see Genesis 37:2–50:26).

This Joseph was a lot like me: the cocky, overconfident younger son of the family. His eleven brothers knew him as their father's favorite who continually received special treatment, so they conspired together to get rid of him. They sold him to slave traders, and to explain his disappearance from the family, they told their dad that a wild animal had mauled and killed him.

By this time, Joseph had already had specific dreams of who he would become in life. But things certainly weren't going as he

envisioned. The slave traders took him into Egypt and sold him to one of the pharaoh's chief political officials, Potiphar. Joseph served Potiphar well and received promotions, but when Potiphar's wife tried to seduce Joseph, he kept his integrity and said no. To punish him, she went to her husband and falsely accused Joseph of rape, resulting in his unjust imprisonment. In prison, Joseph never lost his faith in God's plan for his life and remained a man of integrity, but it seemed the entire world was against him.

His guard became his friend and learned that Joseph had a divine ability to interpret dreams. Eventually Joseph was called on to interpret a dream that had deeply troubled pharaoh. None of pharaoh's wisest consultants had been able to decipher the dream, but Joseph immediately and accurately did so. He foretold of a future time of national abundance followed by a time of great national famine and scarcity. For interpreting his mystifying dream, pharaoh rewarded Joseph and made him second in command, overseeing all of Egypt.

During the prosperous time, Joseph wisely stored up Egypt's abundant harvest as security for the drought ahead. As a result, during the years of starvation, Egypt still had food, so Joseph's starving brothers came there in search of food to keep their families alive. They didn't recognize their younger Hebrew brother, who was now a mature prominent Egyptian from whom they had to buy all their food, but Joseph eventually revealed his true identity. The brothers experienced great remorse for their past actions, and Joseph forgave them. It turned out to be a joyous reunion between an estranged family and a lost son and brother.

When his own brothers sold Joseph into slavery, no doubt he struggled with rejection and fear. And when he was falsely accused and imprisoned, he once again had to feel hopeless. Yet Joseph had an unfair advantage. He had a dream from God.

He relied on God to fulfill his purpose, eventually causing Joseph to save not only a nation from starvation but also his own family. Even though Joseph had every reason to doubt, he didn't. He believed that God was in control of his life, and he remained steadfast as the man God created him to be, in spite of all the unjust difficulties. God honors integrity, obedience, and faithfulness, and with God's help, we can fulfill our purpose.

Joseph became what God created him to be. However, God often creates people for different purposes, even though purposes sometimes appear quite similar. For example, while the Bible clearly states men and women are equal, we are definitely not the same. Let a seven-year-old boy out into the woods, and in no time, he will pick up a stick that will quickly become a prop for a sword or firearm to fight off some imaginary enemy. At the same time, watch the nurturing nature of a seven-year-old girl, who picks up a toy doll and immediately becomes a caring surrogate mom to it. Give most boys the same doll and they will likely pop its head off and use it for target practice. Of course, even among boys and girls, differences exist within those groups. God created everyone for different purposes.

I certainly can illustrate this further using my wife, Kathy, and me as examples. Kathy and I are very different. We're like motorcycles: a Harley is made to go fast, feel cool, and make noise, whereas a moped is also a motorcycle, but it is made to be quiet and efficient. I like to think I'm a Harley—a little wild and dangerous but with a sense of purpose. My wife is the little moped: sometimes she makes an annoying little whining sound, but she's cute, efficient, and so much more dependable. God made each of us uniquely and for a special purpose, and if we want to find contentment in our lives, then we must seek out our *specific* purpose. Anything less is frustration.

I'm reminded of Bowdie, a Golden Retriever we had for ten years. When he was a puppy, we had just bought a big fluffy down-feather comforter for our bed. My wife and Bowdie were both excited about our new purchase but for different reasons. I will never forget Bowdie's eyes when Kathy and I came home to find him standing in a pile of feathers and shredded cloth. He was only living out what he was created to be. Shame on us for putting him in the house with that comforter! But at the end of his life, he was a fat couch potato, far from his bird-hunting bloodline. In fact, if a wild duck had landed on old Bowdie's nose during one of his midday naps, I think he'd have rolled the other way and gotten back to dreaming. Because we never allowed old Bowdie to be that instinctual bird retriever, he became an animal far different from what he was born to be.

I want to be who God created me to be: a warrior and a leader, not a couch potato or anything else. My future might not include me being a warrior on the battlefield, but I can still fight for what's right, and I can be an example for others. All of this is part of building my legacy.

Whenever I meet veterans who are at a low point in their lives, I always try to take them back to the proud moment when they graduated basic training. In my case (and in the case of most warriors), I felt like a superhero when I graduated USMC boot camp. I was on top of the world! I imagined what I would be and do, and I thought about my legacy. But when do warriors lose that moment? When do they forget? When do we lose focus on our legacy? We lose it when we stop fighting. There are always things worth fighting for: your legacy, your honor, your integrity, and even your health. Our roles as men—as husbands, fathers, and leaders—in our communities will bring us to battles that will require us to rise up as warriors and fight. And we must. Discovering the very

CHAPTER 6

YOU KILLED ME

Praise be to the LORD my Rock,
who trains my hands for war,
my fingers for battle.

PSALM 144:1

By the time I completed my first four-year enlistment in the Marine Corps, I had finished all of my initial reconnaissance training and even served as a team leader on several JTF-6 missions (joint task force), focusing on drug-trafficking activity into the United States. I was in love with the job and felt like there was no better fit for me in my profession as a young warrior. On the domestic side, I had been married for two years, and my son, Hunter, had arrived four months before my end of active service date.

With no wars going on in the world at that time and on my low income as a marine corporal, I decided I would transition to the Marine Corps Reserve and get an education. If everything worked out, I would return to active duty as a Marine Corps officer

(otherwise known by the enlisted guys as joining the dark side). I needed a job to provide income to take care of my new family, and being a police officer in the New Orleans area, where I could continue my service as marine reservist at 3rd Force Reconnaissance Company in Mobile, Alabama, suited me well.

While I never had a burning desire to be a police officer, I truly enjoyed it, and in my four-year tenure, I did a variety of jobs. One was working undercover in narcotics. I not only had military experience, but I also had a youthful appearance, so my first assignment was to be a senior in high school. I hadn't liked high school the first time, but at twenty-one, I was back in school, skipping class, going to teenage parties, and buying drugs from adults selling to kids. My *21 Jump Street* adventure ended with forty-plus felony arrests, two on-duty shooting incidents, a few fistfights, and an attempted murder on me personally. I was proud of the positive impact I made, and I earned a good reputation in the department before transitioning to do my time as a patrol officer.

Less than one year into my new duty assignment, I was on night shift when I heard a radio call about a domestic violence disturbance. My buddy, Steve, a seasoned police officer and former Marine Corps Gulf War veteran, took the call. I quickly finished off the last bite of my steak sandwich and began to head his way in case he needed backup. The call ended up being much more than we expected.

As I worked my way toward Steve, I remember the radio traffic being unusually quiet. Then his stressed voice burst over the radio, yelling for additional units. In mid-transmission, Steve's voice cut out, and what we call the Murphy's Law of Combat ensued, except it was not in a combat war zone but rather on the streets of America. It turned out that the entire radio system had a temporary failure, and all radio traffic fell silent.

I stepped on the gas to get there as fast as I could. It seemed that every car in front of me on River Road (which had no shoulder and was parallel to the Mississippi River) stopped on the road because of my lights and sirens. Something in my gut told me Steve needed my help and fast, so I blew my horn and weaved around the traffic. I finally arrived on the scene to a crowd of about thirty people in front of an elevated modular house. I saw Steve engaged in an animated verbal exchange with the lady who appeared to live there.

As I approached, Steve informed me that the lady's husband had barricaded himself in the back room and had a rifle. He said the man wanted to kill his wife, and Steve needed me to get her out of there. I attempted to usher her off the porch, but she immediately began to fight me. So, I did what seemed most logical: I threw her over the rail and told the spectating crowd to get her back, which they did.

Steve drew his weapon and covered the window of the room where the man was barricaded to ensure that he didn't start shooting out the window at his wife or his three children, who were also in the crowd. I took up a position covering the front door, which was wide open and catty-cornered from the hallway that led to the barricaded room. From my position, I noticed a mirror in the hallway through which I got a glimpse of Russell. He was a big man: 6 feet 3 inches, 260 pounds or more, and he was breathing heavily—like a bull getting ready to charge. I saw him holding what appeared to be a hunting rifle and checking the chamber to make sure it was loaded.

I yelled, "Police! Put the gun down!" It didn't faze him.

I tried a new tactic. "Russell, this is serious. We don't want to hurt you. Don't walk out here with that gun. Just put it down and let's talk."

He ignored my commands.

"You need to leave," he said in a strained voice. "I want to talk to my wife."

He turned the corner with the gun, and we looked at each other. Our eyes locked, and I knew at that moment he wasn't going to back down … ever.

The rifle sat on his shoulder in an oddly nonchalant fashion, and his finger was near the trigger. I thought he might be taunting me or seeing how close he could get to me. With Russell pointing the barrel of his rifle directly at me, I had every right to use lethal force and end the standoff, but I chose not to.

Instead, I escalated my commands: "Russell! Stop or I'm going to kill you." (Normal police dialogue was out the window at this point.)

He began walking quickly toward me, saying, "Put down *your* gun."

If someone had asked me that morning what I would have done in this very situation—a gun pointed at me by a guy speed walking toward me—unquestionably my answer would have been that I'd shoot him. But there I was with a man who was playing games with my use-of-force policy. From where I was standing, I could see kids' toys on the floor and family pictures on the wall, and I could hear his wife screaming in the background. Taking a man's life becomes more difficult when you see the people it would affect staring back at you, so I made a quick decision to attempt to disarm him, even though he was nearly a foot taller and 130 pounds heavier.

I lunged forward, grabbing the barrel of his rifle with my left hand while tucking my right hand in tight to retain my service pistol, and then I used a front kick to hit him in the groin. The kick was

hard; I was training heavily in Muay Thai kickboxing at the time. My aim was perfect.

But it didn't faze him a bit. I knew I was now engaged in life-or-death, hand-to-hand combat, and someone could die. I tried another kick, but as I kicked him, he grabbed my right wrist—the one holding my service pistol. I knew I now had no choice but to shoot him. I rolled my wrist over his hand to break his grip, and as my barrel pointed at the center of his chest, I squeezed off a shot and watched it impact center mass. I then fired five more times, center mass. I could also hear Steve's pistol firing right next to my left ear. Everything slowed down.

This was my first gunfight, and I watched, in what felt like slow motion, as the slide of my Glock-22 functioned. It's a strange thing when someone experiences a traumatic event. For the rest of your life, you can remember the smallest details around that incident. Memories become etched into your brain like data that's saved internally to better prepare you for survival in the future. The design of the human mind and body allows both to adapt, survive, and improve; it is quite amazing when you think about it. To this day, I can picture the casings rolling out of the top ejection port. I could even hear the function of the weapons, like slow-motion factory presses stamping out parts on an assembly line. The rounds fired off like firecrackers: there was no loud bang, no ringing ears. My awareness, combined with an eerie sense of calm, heightened to indescribable levels in that short moment. I felt no anxiety.

Steve and I had reacted perfectly, firing twelve shots total, of which eleven impacted. (This later led to a debate between the two of us as to who dropped the one round. It wasn't me, by the way.) Russell, having been hit center mass, did a half turn away from us and hit the ground on his knees. He looked back at me, and our eyes met one more time.

"You killed me," he said. He knew it was the end.

I didn't respond verbally. I tackled him and ripped the rifle away, tossing it aside as I handcuffed him. His opposite arm, which wasn't holding the rifle, must have been in front of his chest as he was hit because the .40 caliber hollow points had blown out the bones in his wrist. It felt like a limp noodle, and while the gunshot wounds to his body did not bleed much, his mangled arm bled profusely.

As I patted him down for other weapons, I felt something slippery and noticed I was covered in blood from my hands to elbows. As I lay on top of Russell, I heard him exhale and felt his life leave his body. It's a feeling I will never forget.

I had dealt with death before, both of loved ones and friends. When my brother was murdered, I was fourteen years old, and it impacted me in a profound and painful way. But taking someone's life for the first time gave me an immediate perspective of just how permanent death is.

I will never forget the way Russell's wife screamed. Bystanders in the crowd held her back as she fought to get to me, or maybe to him, but she was hysterical and in anguish. I also saw the children held back by people in the crowd. Steve and I cleared the rest of the house, and other officers swarmed in to take control and assist. I looked around and saw a family's home: the family pictures, the toys, and the table where they ate dinner together. I scrubbed Russell's blood off my arms in the kitchen sink; it seemed impossible to get it all off.

In the following weeks and months, we faced media criticism. I stood before a grand jury who examined whether a second-degree murder indictment should apply, but Steve and I were cleared. Later, we both received Louisiana's highest law-enforcement medal for bravery: The Medal of Valor.[7]

The ceremony was strange, and it was difficult to feel proud. I was thankful Steve and I were alive and that no innocent persons had been killed, but I was also angry with Russell for forcing me to kill him. I believe a piece of me died that night right beside Russell, perhaps not forever but certainly for several years to follow. My struggles after this incident stemmed largely from my lack of maturity and understanding of what had happened, why it happened, and especially how I was supposed to deal with it.

On one hand, I was angry that Russell had made me kill him in front of his family; on the other hand, I didn't feel badly about it. Whether it was the accolades of my fellow officers, my joy for surviving, or the thrill of the event, as crazy as it sounds, I wanted to engage in and survive a hand-to-hand battle again. I even began seeking out these types of altercations and pushing the envelope in every encounter with a "bad guy." I wanted to provoke life-and-death circumstances.

But at the same time, I began to question myself, thinking that something must be wrong with me because I didn't feel badly and wanted to relive the moment. I must be an evil and murderous person. I began to judge and even fear myself. I couldn't understand my feelings, but I was certain that I wasn't going to share them with anyone. For years, I battled this alone in my mind, thinking I committed some "eternal sin" through my actions that night.

Years later, after Afghanistan, I found myself continuing to ask the same question of my motives and my heart. *Had I become a monster?* Today, I know the answer, and I know that I am a whole man again. I did my duty, loved my country, and I am proud to have had the privilege to protect innocent human lives. But accepting the hard truths that helped me reach that conclusion wasn't easy.

Now that I'm on the other side of my own struggles and working with other veterans and police officers, I see clearly that I'm not alone in this inner battle of self-judgment and personal worth. Many warriors I speak with have the same thoughts I had—not the survivor's guilt, or "poor me," or "I'm so shaken up by all the killing that I'm seeing faces of dead bad guys in my sleep." Rather, the questions and concerns that they need to work through are usually:

- *Why don't I feel bad about killing? I expected to feel bad but didn't. Where was my empathy? Am I a monster?*
- *I'm evil. How can I be a good husband or father?*
- *Without a war, I have no purpose.*
- *If my family knew what I have done, they would think badly of me.*

These thoughts are common with guys who have been in the trenches and put lead down a two-way range. They did what their training taught them to do.

Let's not sugarcoat it. What is it that the army and marines train young infantrymen to do? Kill people and destroy things. Period. No need to make it sound pleasant. A young infantryman must be able to kill, and when he does, he can't just pack it up and go home. He needs to wake up tomorrow and do it again. Why? Because war is ugly. It results in someone's death, and the infantryman knows, *It's better him than me or my buddy.* It starts in day one of boot camp: the mental conditioning to prepare the warrior to pull that trigger, toss that grenade, or call in that fire support to take others' lives away from them. Whether reluctantly or willingly, the question will always surface in the heart and soul of every warrior who has done such deeds: *Was this just?*

We can find an answer to this question in the many Bible

stories where God had men kill others to carry out his will. If all killing equates to the specific murder that the Ten Commandments forbids, then God would be violating his own commands when he tells us to kill. Yet, when we look closely, not all killing is the same.

The Hebrew translation for the word *kill* that appears in the Ten Commandments of our English Bible literally means "to murder"; that is, to unjustly shed innocent blood. This is quite different from other uses of the word *kill* in the Bible. For example, in 1 Samuel 15:3, God told King Saul to go and kill all the people of Amalek. The Hebrew word translated *kill* here literally means to "take the life of." Our English translations of the original words used in Hebrew do not always capture their full meanings.

One approach that can offer perspective is to consider the instances where God blessed those who *did* kill others and who did so according to the rules he laid down. The life of an Old Testament leader named Samson provides a clear example of this. He was a judge anointed by God to govern the nation of Israel. Blessed with astounding physical strength, he was an amazing warrior. In fact, in one battle, he himself killed one thousand Philistines—all with the jawbone of a donkey, and he only stopped killing because he got thirsty! Today, people would probably call him a beast.

As amazing a warrior as he was, at the end of his life, the very nation Samson was supposed to defend his people from forced him into servitude. Because he violated clear directions that God had given him, Samson lost his great strength, had his eyes gouged out by his captors, and was chained to the column of a public building so that those who attended a party could make fun of this once-powerful man who had become a slave. As his Philistine enemies ridiculed him, Samson prayed to God for his strength to return so that he could bring judgment to those in

the building. God answered his prayer, and Samson pulled the building down on himself and everyone attending the party, killing thousands of his nation's oppressors. The Bible tells us that Samson killed more people in his final act than he had during the rest of his life. This is an amazing story of God answering a prayer and enabling someone to do the work of judgment by killing the nation's enemy.

The biblical account of Samson appears in Judges 16, but we can also look earlier in the same book (chapter 3) and read about another leader who killed according to God's rules. God used Ehud, a.k.a. "The Left-Handed Assassin," to free his people. Yes, the Bible has a story of an assassin, and guess what? He was a man of God commissioned by God to kill an evil dictator. Didn't learn that one in Sunday school after singing "This Little Light of Mine," did you?

Evil Moabite King Eglon had enslaved the children of Israel and kept them for eighteen years. He was a physically massive man, and he was no friend to God. In fact, he represented the worst of all that is bad about those who reject God. Ehud, who was left-handed, prepared an eighteen-inch-long dagger to slay the king. At this time, to be left-handed was unusual, so when he went to meet with King Eglon, Eglon's bodyguards would look for a weapon but find none because they would look on the wrong side.

The king had granted Ehud, who claimed to have a secret message to give him, a private audience. When the two were alone together, the Bible tells us, "As the king rose from his seat, Ehud reached with his left hand, drew the sword from his right thigh and plunged it into the king's belly." This was a violent death. Ehud was not messing around. "Even the handle sank in after the blade, and his bowels discharged. Ehud did not pull the sword out, and the fat closed in over it. Then Ehud went out to the porch;

he shut the doors of the upper room behind him and locked them" (Judges 3:20–23).

Ehud had executed the perfect hit. He slipped out the back door, locking his victim inside. The guards and servants didn't look for him right away. The Bible says they were embarrassed while waiting to check on the king because they thought he was on the toilet. But when they realized something was wrong, they finally located a key to open the room, finding their king dead on the floor, and Ehud, the left-handed assassin judge, long gone from the scene.

Ehud gathered the Israelites to share the news, but the killing was not over. "'Follow me,' [Ehud] ordered, 'for the LORD has given Moab, your enemy, into your hands.' So they followed him down and took possession of the fords of the Jordan that led to Moab; they allowed no one to cross over. At that time, they struck down about ten thousand Moabites, all vigorous and strong; not one escaped. That day Moab was made subject to Israel, and the land had peace for eighty years" (vv. 28–30).

Throughout Scripture, we find dozens of examples just like these. They allow us to better understand that killing and murder are not the same. I believe deeply that anyone who has killed and has intimately witnessed death up close and personal not only knows the difference but can also *feel* that difference deep inside his or her soul. There is no glory in killing people. Innocent family members often become collateral damage and suffer, whether physically, mentally, or spiritually. Yet in this broken and evil world, the need always exists for brave warriors who represent God's values and purposes to stand in the face of evil and strike it down for the sake of defending the innocent.

Some people will try to mislead others by saying that God and Christians should not "hate" and that it would be an eternal

sin to kill. But this is not accurate. For those very few who will have the unpleasant experience of taking another's life, there is an unfair advantage in knowing that God not only hates evil but will also, from time to time, use men to dispatch that evil in the just and right defense of others.

I am keenly aware that we, as warriors, are vulnerable to being sucked into a moment when we risk crossing the line between killing and murder. We could cross that line through the fog of war—moments of rage, passion, and hate. Sometimes we cross that line, and we become the very monsters we fight against, and we know when that occurs. God knows this, too, but thankfully, we serve a loving and forgiving God—a God who loves and honors his warriors. As the apostle Paul explained in Romans 8:1–2: "Therefore, there is now no condemnation for those who are in Christ Jesus, because through Christ Jesus the law of the Spirit who gives life has set you free from the law of sin and death." There will always be an unfair advantage for the warrior who understands God's grace and will for our lives.

CHAPTER 7

THE CAPTAIN
OF THE *TITANIC*

A happy heart makes the face cheerful,
but heartache crushes the spirit.

PROVERBS 15:13

As comfortable as my team and I had become living among the local populous of Kabul, there were always reminders that we were still in Afghanistan and that any moment could be our last if we didn't stay sharp. "Stay alert, stay alive" was a phrase I tried to live by. Staying alive in that community required us to vary our travel routes, with irregular departure and arrival times so as not to create predictable patterns and thus become a victim of a kidnapping or ambush.

With so much training and awareness, it's still difficult to avoid becoming numb in even the harshest environments. The bottom line is that complacency kills. It is something you have to fight minute by minute so that it never takes root, or it will literally

kill you. From time to time, it was hard not to lower my guard and allow that complacency to creep in anyway.

One morning, I awoke and went downstairs for a cup of coffee. Bink always woke up first and usually had a full pot of coffee in his own system. In fact, I think Bink was 100 percent fueled on caffeine and Copenhagen dipping tobacco. Just three of us lived in the house at the time. Dano and I said our casual good mornings as Bink polished off his final cup of joe.

As he casually sipped his coffee, without a care in the world, he said, "Morning! You guys hear that rocket shoot across the backyard?"

I replied, "Whatever, Bink. No one shot a rocket!"

Bink continued to sip his coffee. "Okay, dude. Don't believe me."

Dano and I joked that he was either messing with us or losing his mind. Bink had a tendency to become paranoid at times (which was justifiable in those circumstances), but that morning he had a super chill demeanor.

As I sipped my own coffee, I ventured out into our front courtyard and ran into our gate security guard. (It is customary for most people in Kabul, especially foreigners, to have a local security guard at their front gate.) The guard approached me, overly excited, and tried to communicate in a combination of Dari and broken English that a rocket had hit the house down the street. As he pointed out the damage over our fence, Bink stood behind me and said, "Told you, dude!" What a crazy place! Someone had literally shot a rocket over our yard, and I slept through it, and Bink wasn't fazed a bit. It hit me right then that maybe we'd been there too long.

Shortly after the morning's excitement, we received the task of providing support to other members of our task force. They had received a green light for a short-fused operation and needed a

specific vehicle for it. It's no secret that special operations teams often use local vehicles for unconventional warfare in order to blend into the local environment and culture of the combat theater. We needed a van with valid papers and permits so that we could access a particular area. We also wanted something with a little Afghan-bling but still inconspicuous. For obvious reasons, it had to have certain add-ons, like window coverings.

We had the means to get it done quickly, so we got rolling right away to find a vehicle. After some searching, we found the perfect van. I had one of my "terps" (interpreters) take it to town and quickly add a few bells and whistles while also making sure it was in working mechanical order before we delivered it to our boys.

We coordinated a delivery point two hours away, and Dano, Bink, and I headed out to do the handoff. I drove one of our lifted Toyota Hilux trucks. Bink was in another Hilux since he was going to stay at the delivery point. And the little Haji van (*Haji* refers to a dedicated Muslim who's been to Mecca) was driven by Dano, which was ironic because he's a giant of a man. It's definitely not the vehicle most people would imagine seeing a burly, bearded warrior drive, so it was a hilarious sight. His long dark hair and thick beard made him look like a medieval warrior who should have been carrying a giant battle-ax instead of an M-4 carbine. The design of the van made it even more comical. With the engine in the center, the driver is forced to the very front, essentially sitting on the dashboard. So, the picture of Dano sitting that way was nothing short of ridiculous and reminded me of a scene from a cartoon.

I led the way as we headed out of Kabul to our delivery point in the desert. The road had no shoulder and was not wide enough for two vehicles. According to the locals, both sides of the road were littered with mines that the Russians had dropped after

they invaded Afghanistan in 1979, alongside many other roads throughout the country, to prevent ambushes on their convoys. The locals stacked rocks near every mined area that they found and painted one side of the stack white to indicate particularly dangerous locations. Children avoided those stacks as naturally as kids in the States avoid playing in the street. Despite their effort to identify dangerous areas, many local kids lost limbs and even died from their mine-laden countryside.

Aside from the risk of driving off the road and into a mine-field, the Taliban, and even criminal thugs, commonly staged fake police checkpoints in order to rob travelers or kidnap foreigners. We planned to maintain a constant speed of 75 kph (45 mph) without making stops for anyone.

Still leading the way, I could see in my rearview mirror that Bink was in the rear, and Dano bounced along behind me in his little Haji wagon—quite a sight for sure. Then something else caught my eye: I saw a pristine Mercedes Benz sedan with tinted windows approaching at well over 100 kph, coming up right behind Bink. It caught me off guard because it was so out of place. It was like I had just spotted a two-carat diamond in the middle of a pile of dog poop.

The sedan flashed its lights and used its blinker to signal us to move over, a common use of blinkers in Afghanistan. We all shifted right to let the car zoom past us. As it passed me, I marveled at the luxury sedan, but my amusement came to an end when I saw the sedan dodge a big rock in the middle of the road ahead. I wasn't about to swerve off the road into one of those minefields, and I did not even have time to think about it, so I took my foot off the gas, centered my Hilux, and braced for impact.

Nothing.

Because of the elevated suspension on the truck, I didn't

even ding the rock. But before I could breathe a sigh of relief, I remembered that Dano was right on my six, flying along at 75 kph. I looked in my rearview mirror just in time to see him crash our new assault wagon. The little Haji van turned a full 90 degrees and ended up perpendicular to our direction of travel. It had to have been at least four feet in the air. That image in my rearview mirror is frozen in my mind forever. It seemed inevitable that Dano would either roll or go off into the minefield—or both. Amazingly, neither happened. While the van landed nearly 90 degrees sideways, it miraculously bounced back, landed straight on its wheels, and then screeched to a halt.

Bink and I stopped our trucks and quickly got out with our M-4 rifles, unsure if this was some sort of staged ambush. Thankfully, no attack came. Silence greeted us in that open desert—until we heard steam hissing from the smashed radiator. A strong smell of smoke filled the air from worn-out brakes and melted tire rubber. As we waited for Dano to step out, we could see that he was white as a ghost. The moment we knew Dano was fine, Bink and I were on the asphalt almost unable to breathe from laughing so hard. It was one of those rare moments that breaks the tension of reality, and we couldn't stop laughing. Poor Dano was in complete shock yet grateful to be alive with only a busted nose and a small cut on his forehead.

The undercarriage of the vehicle looked as if a hook had ripped its centerline from bumper to bumper. The dashboard, where the radio used to be, had apparently gone into a black hole, and the steering wheel where Dano had braced for his life had been sheered in half but thankfully hadn't impaled his body. We had to abandon the vehicle there, which meant postponing the operation. Some lucky bad guy got a pass that night, but I have no doubt he got his later.

I know this book has some heavy chapters, but so does life. There are times in the midst of the most serious situations, and even the most tragic, when we have to pause and laugh for a moment, embracing even the smallest moments of joy, humor, and bliss. I wanted to do that by sharing the moment when Dano's new nickname became "The Captain of the *Titanic*" for having found an iceberg in the middle of the Taliban-infested desert of Afghanistan.

For years after the incident, whenever I needed to muster a smile for a photo, I would simply recall the image of Dano, crammed in that tiny Haji van and floating through the air to certain death, in my rearview mirror. As I've learned more about God, I've also come to learn that he never says, "Thou shalt *not* have fun nor smile in all thy days." Having a good time in and of itself is not a sin. In fact, I'm absolutely certain that God has a sense of humor and takes pleasure in us finding joy during moments of stress and anguish, especially when we can freely do so because of our confidence that he is in control. If God didn't have a sense of humor, why would he use a talking donkey? (Read this in Numbers 22:21–39.)

Not unlike the talking donkey in the movie *Shrek*, Balaam's donkey had the gift of gab. In this Bible story, a prophet named Balaam was on a serious mission, riding to an important meeting. While headed down the road, he came upon an angry angel that had drawn its sword. The donkey saw the angel and the imminent danger and immediately stopped and laid down rather than risk encountering the armed angel. But Balaam didn't see the angel and tried to make the donkey go forward. It wouldn't. Three times Balaam proceeded to beat the heck out of the donkey, trying to make it move. Finally, the angel allowed the donkey to speak, and the donkey and Balaam then had a passive-aggressive conversation about why Balaam was such a jerk. The angel, with its drawn sword, then revealed itself to Balaam and chastised him for hitting

the donkey, informing him that if the donkey had not stopped and laid down, the angel would have killed Balaam. Why? No idea, but it was a close call for Balaam and a good call by the donkey.

Of course, God's humor is never cruel in the way that humans twist it to be at times. God is entirely pure and untainted; therefore so is his humor, and it has a positive effect. As the author of Proverbs wrote, "A happy heart makes the face cheerful" (15:13), and "Light in a messenger's eyes brings joy to the heart" (v. 30). And Proverbs 16:24 adds, "Gracious words are a honeycomb, sweet to the soul and healing to the bones."

Aren't you glad we can all take some time to laugh? Even in the worst or most serious of times. I'm thankful for the many moments of laughter and joy that I shared with my brothers during my service in the military and throughout life in general. I believe an unfair advantage is gained by those who know and believe that God is ultimately in control. They can embrace the fact that regardless of how serious, tragic, or important a situation may seem to us, there are also moments when it is okay to let go, smile, and laugh.

CHAPTER 8

OUT OF CONTROL

I will give you a new heart and put a new spirit in you;
I will remove from you your heart of stone
and give you a heart of flesh.

EZEKIEL 36:26

The longer I was in Afghanistan, the thinner my patience became. Everything set me off. I was a bit of a madman, extremely intense about everything, which was okay and at times even necessary. But it was not beneficial when I took that attitude home with me. How was I supposed to operate in a hostile environment under overwhelming stress, driven with intensity one day, then go home the next and become Mr. Rogers: husband, father, and friendly neighbor? I didn't have a switch to flip for that.

On one of my trips home from Afghanistan, a teammate, Dave, and I went into the city together to have a meeting with one of the upper-echelon GS (government service) DoD staffers, who had oversight of our task force. After a debriefing in our home base sensitive compartmentalized information facility (SCIF), all

of us went out for a nice dinner, spent the evening socializing, and then called it a night. Dave and I were heading north out of the city on a major interstate, and the rain poured so hard that we probably shouldn't have been going the 70-plus mph we were.

Suddenly, I saw a full-sized Chevy truck coming out of the median and across the interstate completely perpendicular to the flow of traffic. I slammed on the brakes and swerved, just missing the truck, but the small car next to me smashed into the Chevy broadside without braking. It was a full speed impact, and the car crushed like a soda can. My immediate thought was, *An entire family just died in that car!* Cars stopped on the interstate, and people rushed to help.

The truck, however, began to move forward to get away. The car had hit the truck in the extended cab and bed, and although the driver's side was smashed in, it was still drivable. The man driving the truck sped off.

I have a problem when people run away; I can't help but instinctively chase. The occupants of the smashed car had plenty of help, but I wasn't going to let that truck get away. I followed him while Dave, in the passenger seat, dialed 911. The man exited the interstate onto a country road. I followed, flashing my lights for him to stop, while Dave updated the 911 dispatcher.

A few miles down the road, the man pulled into a gas station and stopped next to the pumps. Dave gave the location to the dispatcher, and I parked far away because I was raging. I wanted to break this guy's skull open for killing the occupants of that car and nearly killing me and my friend. When we got out of my vehicle, Dave yelled at the guy, "Stay here! The police are on their way!"

The man, now out of his truck, exited the passenger door because of the damage to the driver's side. He yelled back at us, "Look at my truck! Someone hit me and ran!"

I replied, "I saw what happened, and the police are coming." I still kept my distance from the guy because I was on the brink of losing it.

I called my wife, Kathy, on my cell phone to let her know of the delay, and I heard the man yelling at me, "Who are you talking to? You should mind your business!" I tried my hardest to stay calm.

Robert E. Howard, author of *Conan the Barbarian*, once said, "Civilized men are more discourteous than savages because they know they can be impolite without having their skulls split, as a general thing."[8] Maybe because I was in a suit and tie, the man assumed I was a civilized individual. What he didn't know was that at that time in my life, I wasn't a civilized man; I was a savage. I was a time bomb on the constant brink of exploding.

The man began to walk toward me, and I warned him, "Stay by your truck, or I'm going to hurt you!" I put my phone in my suit coat pocket and thought I had hung it up. However, I hadn't, so Kathy was now an audio spectator of the events about to unfold.

As the man approached me, I think he believed we were going to get into a verbal argument or maybe a shoving match like kids at a park. But as soon as he was within arm's reach, I grabbed him and launched him off the ground, his feet flying over his head. The back of his head hit the asphalt first. I landed in a solid Brazilian jiu-jitsu mount position, and he wasn't going to get up. Just as I was about to smash his head in with my elbows, Dave yelled at me to stop, and I did. Dave saved this man (at least for the moment). He was still trying to get up, but he had no clue how to escape the mount position. I grabbed a handful of his hair, poked my finger against his forehead, and chewed him out. I stood up, shoved him by his face, and then backed away.

He stood up and then challenged me: "Try that again!"

I was momentarily composed, so I didn't. I informed him that

in a few minutes he'd be going to jail, and I would wave goodbye and laugh at him when he did. He didn't like that possibility, so he ran for his truck, saying he was leaving.

Like I said, if it runs, I chase it, and I did. He went in through the passenger door and started his truck. I stood in the door well on the passenger side and told him to shut it off. He cursed at me, slammed his truck into gear, and stomped on the gas pedal. I jumped in with him.

We were accelerating across the parking lot, and as I tried to put the truck in park, he kept swatting my hand. That's when the time bomb went off. I went savage. I grabbed his hair and jammed his head into the door well. With a good elevated position, I started dropping right-crosses into the side of his face—hard. After I landed several blows, I heard him make a gargling noise. I threw the truck in park, and the gears grinded us to a stop.

He was still making noises but not moving. His eye was split open and bleeding profusely. I was seeing red at this point and trying to pull him out of the truck, but he was stuck behind the steering wheel. Dave saved him once again, telling me to leave him alone and just take his keys. I pulled them from the ignition and threw them as far as I could into the neighboring woods.

When the police finally showed up, the man jumped out of the truck and suddenly acted the victim. He told the officer that I was a crazy man who tried to kill him. The officer took my statement and arrested the man. As promised, I waved and laughed as he went off to jail that night.

Fortunately, the accident he had caused did not kill anyone. The occupant of the other car was a lady, and she was alone. Medical personnel airlifted her from the accident scene. (I met her at the trial where the man pled guilty and received a steep sentence.) I am thankful that no one got hurt in the accident that

night, and I am also thankful that I didn't seriously hurt anyone, which was Kathy's concern too.

I justified my actions that night as, "I did my citizen duty within the confines of law." I didn't want that man to leave the scene and hurt someone else. While I would do the same thing today if I had to, my heart is now in a completely different place than it was during those dark times when I was often out of control and dangerous to myself and others.

On another trip home, I made it back in time to celebrate the birthday of my little girl, Haili. It was a big deal for her, and she was so excited that her daddy could be there. But when Haili said she didn't like the icing on the cake, I instantly flew into a rage, grabbed a handful of the cake, and threw it against the wall in front of everyone. With my outburst of uncontrolled anger, I had destroyed my little girl's special day. *Who does that?* I knew I was a raging lunatic, and my wife and kids feared me.

When I started down that path of anger, I was out of control. I had no brakes to stop it, and I was more comfortable spending time in Afghanistan than being home with my family. But I wasn't only acting out in rage with my family or reckless drivers; it was happening in all areas of my life.

As Uncle Ben told Peter Parker in *Spider-Man*, "With great power comes great responsibility." I know that I possess the ability, knowledge, and physical strength to hurt people. I am wired to do so, and I'm capable of doing it. I've done it both in the military and in martial arts, but with that great power comes a great responsibility, especially the need for control. The awareness that I didn't have full control of myself scared me. I had power but was not exercising it responsibly.

On several occasions in the Bible, we see that Jesus exercised great power, and he always used great responsibility with it.

On one occasion, he returned to his hometown and took part in a meeting at the local synagogue. Initially, the people were pleasantly amazed by his teachings, but then he addressed a controversial topic that didn't sit well with his listeners: "All the people in the synagogue were furious…They got up, drove him out of the town, and took him to the brow of the hill on which the town was built, in order to throw him off the cliff" (Luke 4:28–29).

Imagine the scene: Jesus was backed onto the edge of a cliff, surrounded by folks from his hometown. They were angry and intended to kill him for what he had said. What he did next always amazes me: "But he walked right through the crowd and went on his way" (v. 30). How can Jesus simply walk through the middle of an angry crowd and go untouched on his way? My imagination comes up with one definite possibility: Jesus was probably a physically intimidating man. After all, he did manual labor working as a carpenter, and some estimates calculate that he walked more than twenty thousand miles in his short thirty-three years on earth, with over thirty-five hundred of those miles during his three-year public ministry. Jesus wasn't a pretty boy with an artsy white robe and long silky hair blowing gently in the breeze. No, I think it's pretty obvious that Jesus was probably a physical beast. So when the crowd cornered him on the edge of that cliff and he turned and faced them with those callused hands and big carpenter forearms, no one wanted to touch him. They backed down, and he simply walked off.

But even when Jesus got angry, he still controlled his strength and power. In John 2, we see an angry Jesus: "Jesus went up to Jerusalem. In the temple courts he found people selling cattle, sheep and doves, and others sitting at tables exchanging money. So he made a whip out of cords, and drove all from the temple courts, both sheep and cattle; he scattered the coins of the

money changers and overturned their tables. To those who sold doves he said, 'Get these out of here! Stop turning my Father's house into a market!'" (John 2:13–16).

Jesus witnessed what was taking place and was definitely unhappy. He got angry. He saw something that he knew was dead wrong—something about which he had a deep passion and conviction. He wasn't passive about what he saw, and he wasn't about to let it happen on his watch. He didn't avoid physical conflict here but rather initiated it, yet he definitely did *not* react in rage. As he considered his plan of attack, he stopped, paused, and then deliberately "made a whip out of cords" (v. 15). Jesus didn't simply grab the closest thing to him and start swinging in a fit of temper like I did that night on the highway. Instead, his action was premeditated: he took the time to make himself a whip.

Jesus was on a mission, and when he entered the temple courts, he took direct action, creating sheer panic. Imagine the crowds, shoulder to shoulder in a busy temple (the literal house of God inside of which they had wrongly turned into a commercial market), as a wild man came in snapping a whip, driving the sheep and cattle into a panic, and stampeding them. He then flipped the money changers' tables and scattered their coins. The scene had to be pure chaos.

If this were to happen in any market today, everyone would have their cell phone out either to dial 911 or record the drama for social media. Jesus was angry, but while he had the ability to crush everyone and everything there, he remained poised and in complete control: "To those who sold doves he said, 'Get these out of here! Stop turning my Father's house into a market!'" (v. 16). Jesus understood that the doves were helpless in their cages, so he didn't show the same aggression as he had with the sheep, cattle, and money changers. He demanded the vendors

remove the doves to protect them from harm. He was powerful, passionate, intentional, and controlled.

In an excerpt from *Beautiful Outlaw*, John Eldredge described this scene at the temple:

> Jesus is a locomotive, a juggernaut. For all practical purposes here, He is the bull in the china shop. . .This is our Jesus. But is this the Jesus of our worship songs? The religious fog sneaks in to obscure Jesus with lines comparing him to, "a rose trampled on the ground." Helpless, lovely Jesus. Vegetarian, pacifist, tranquil. Oh, wait—that was Gandhi. Not Jesus. Can you picture Gandhi or Buddha storming into the polling place of a local election, shouting, overturning tables, sending the participants fleeing? Now throw a small carnival into the mix, which they also need to rout. Impossible. Whoever did this would have to be really committed to clear the building. Fierce and intentional.[9]

The enemy doesn't want us to know this Jesus, but the true Jesus is the model for us all. He is the One who demonstrates both passion and poise for every situation we will face in life. It's okay for us to stand up for what is right—and we must—but in those moments, we must handle our strength with responsibility. In my case, what I did to stop that man from getting on that road again was just. What Jesus did in the temple was just. The difference is what was in our hearts.

The proper boundary line has already been sewn into your heart and soul by God himself, the Creator of warriors and all of mankind. And if you fully trust him and stay on the right side of that line, then you will have an unfair advantage in becoming

the warrior he created you to be: a warrior filled with passion, strength, and control, fully equipped to find victory in the battles ahead.

CHAPTER 9

TRADING MY BIRTHRIGHT

I lift up my eyes to the mountains—
where does my help come from?
My help comes from the LORD,
the Maker of heaven and earth.

PSALM 121:1–2

T hree years had passed since I was last in Afghanistan, and I was now in a different kind of fight. I stood in the center of the MMA cage anxiously awaiting the *StrikeForce* announcer to reveal the results of the only split decision of my fighting career. My mind raced. I virtually heard a drumroll in my head as I knew the fight was close. *Never leave it to the judges*, I thought.

Humberto Deleon and I had put on a show for the screaming fans that filled the ten thousand seats in the Houston Toyota Center. It was the big stage at one of the highest pro-level MMA organizations. I had gone into the fight with a perfect undefeated professional record, having submitted all my previous opponents.

Humberto was a highly-touted rising professional with amazing striking skills. As an accomplished grappler, I had faced interviewers leading up to the fight who questioned my ability to stand and strike with Humberto, and my ego got the best of me. I tried to prove my ability to take the center of the cage and trade punches and kicks with him. We literally beat the heck out of each other for three rounds. I remember landing some great Muay Thai "teep" kicks that hit Humberto flush in the face, but just when I felt confident, I found myself sitting on my butt! I didn't even feel myself get hit, but I did, and I had been knocked down for the first time in my career.

Humberto sensed blood in the water and swarmed me, and I recall a moment of clarity thinking, *How can this be happening to me?* Knowing he had knocked me down made me angry. I knew it was time to turn it up. I abandoned all technique, got up, and started fighting with every bit of aggression I could muster. I wanted the win so badly. Getting knocked down was one thing, but staying down was never an option.

As the referee raised my hand and the announcer declared me the winner, I felt like a champion once again. There I was on top of the world, on the big stage, looking like a rock star. Yet, only moments later, reality would come back to me.

Thousands of fans attended the fight, but my wife was nowhere to be found. Outside the *StrikeForce* cage and beyond the lights, Kathy and I were separated, and my family was facing a terrible divorce. This was the new and relevant fight in which I was engaged. I had been knocked down in life and in marriage, yet I wasn't willing to get up or fight back. When I look back, that moment is a sad reflection of what was most important in my life at the time. I was willing to fight with everything inside of me to get up from Humberto's devastating right hand, to press on and win

for one more notch on my record. *Yet, why was I not willing to fight with the same passion and ferocity for my wife and family?* For my own health and the legacy I'd leave behind. *Why?*

I once heard Brazilian jiu-jitsu master Renzo Gracie say, "People often see fighting as an ugly thing that denigrates the human being. In reality, you see fighting in everything, no matter what it is. Upon waking up in the morning, getting out of bed is a fight, believe it. So, the will to fight is actually the best thing a man can have in his soul." I've always been a fighter, and I believe deeply that, as men, we were born to fight. It's God's design for us, yet at the pinnacle of my career as a professional fighter, I wasn't fighting for the things that mattered most.

Years before I stepped into that cage in the Toyota Center, I had found myself in a dark place, knocked down by life, Afghanistan, and a long history of hardship. However, the downward spiral of my life and marriage wasn't the direct result of the historical incidents of my life but of the way I responded to those incidents and where I went to cope, seek comfort, or even escape my feelings.

In my own experience and in observing other broken people, one of the most common pitfalls is that they chase the wrong gods to fill the hole in their hearts. Sadly, I must admit that I tried to fill that God-shaped hole in my own heart with everything but him—a square peg in a round hole. Being as stubborn as I am, I tried to make life work my way, and continued frustration met me. My Force Recon marine, square-peg-in-a-round-hole, sledgehammer mentality didn't work this time, and I continued to come up empty as false idols, gods, and short-lived satisfactions left me feeling hopeless and incomplete.

When I came home from my last deployment, I was completely broken. One day I was the golden boy of an elite military special operations task force, doing what I believed to be the most

important mission in the War on Terror, and the next, I was benched: diagnosed with severe PTSD, pulled out of the fight and out of my role as a warrior, and removed from my team. I felt devastated.

Besides the destruction of my pride, the removal crushed my dreams of accomplishing the mission, and struggling with a mix of shame, guilt, and overwhelming panic left me in bad shape. I felt that if I honestly expressed my feelings, they would put me in a straitjacket and lock me in a padded room. The idea of being institutionalized for a mental deficiency terrified me. I felt as if I were losing all sanity and would either crack mentally or my body would stop functioning and I would die. Panic attacks became the new norm. For the prior year, I had bottled up the anxiety, stress, and fears that were building up from my work, but they had finally overtaken me, and I crashed. When the floor came out from under me, I had a giant hole inside me. At that time, I didn't know that the void in my heart was a God-shaped hole that nothing else would fill.

While working with other warriors who struggle in the same way, I can see that hole so clearly now. I observe as warriors and their spouses try everything but God to fill that hole. These efforts to fill that void often make things worse—much worse. You can't pour enough liquor, dump enough pills, or throw enough women, fame, fortune, adventure, or success at it. A God-shaped hole is reserved for one thing, and that is Jesus Christ alone. Without him, there will always be emptiness, a longing desire, an unquenchable thirst, an itch never scratched, a hole never filled. I was no different. After getting medications prescribed to numb the anxiety, I, too, tried to find something to fill that void—all the wrong things. When we don't fill our hearts through a soul-level connection with our Creator, we miss being who he created us to be and, ultimately, trade our purpose and legacy for something far less.

For my entire life, I have grappled and trained martial arts and

Brazilian jiu-jitsu. Today I'm a third-degree black belt under Carlson Gracie Jr. and have been blessed to train under the Brazilian jiu-jitsu and mixed martial arts greats like Vinicius "Draculino" Magalhaes, UFC legend Randy Couture, and many others. When I came home from Afghanistan, I had already fought professionally and had gone undefeated, so I had a head start on getting plugged into a new chapter in life. I could be the "cool guy" again! I wanted respect so badly so that I could rebuild that ego I lost on some mountain on the other side of the world. As a result, Kathy and I opened a Brazilian jiu-jitsu/mixed martial arts school and ran it as a family business. We were living the American dream. What we didn't know was that I was not in a position to handle the success that would come with it. I was still broken, not healed by God, and certainly walking outside of the will he had for my life.

The school's success was incredible. We opened with one hundred and eighty students, and in three years, we had one of the biggest Gracie Barra schools in America with an enrollment of approximately nine hundred students in two locations. I had received my black belt in Brazil, had won a mixed martial arts world championship under the *Legacy FC* banner, was undefeated as a pro, and was top ranked in my division (#6 Flyweight and #20 Bantamweight world ranked).[10] I had the world in the palm of my hand, and everything seemed perfect. Well, not so much. In reality, that was the furthest thing from the truth.

Although on the surface everything looked perfect, my life was a train wreck. I was living a lie. Instead of liquor or excessive drug use, I had isolated myself in a fake world of success. I was a mess, and I was angry. My house was not a happy place, and my wife and kids were frightened of me. Kathy and I lived separate lives in our own home; our marriage was dead. My wife and I were worlds apart, and it didn't take long for temptation to overtake me

as I did something I never thought I would do. I turned outside of my marriage for attention and into adultery with other women, and those affairs led to separation from Kathy and my family. I was facing the reality of a devastating divorce.

On top of that, I was living in shame as I still felt as if I had failed at my mission and didn't even want to speak of my past military service. My mental health condition terrified me as I had continued panic attacks or sleepless nights, so I ran from those fears by keeping myself as busy as possible. I had put myself in a position of zero accountability, in a world where everyone lifts you up and tells you what you want to hear but no one tells you what you need to hear. I had chased and caught a false god of success, and it was unfulfilling. The temporary high of a moment in the spotlight not only allowed the void to remain but also caused it to grow.

The path of martial arts is a good one; I love martial arts, and I'm still involved with it today. When I have a bad day at the office, I love nothing more than to get on those mats, find some eighteen-year-old stud, and choke him out. It always makes my day better. However, we can abuse good medicine, and I did that with martial arts; I used it out of context. Like many things in my life, I used worldly endeavors in an attempt to fill a void in my life that only God could fill. Once again, my attempts left me empty and hopeless, even at the top of my MMA career. Instead of dealing with my pain in an appropriate way, I decided to take the easy way out. Many people don't fulfill God's destiny for them because it is too hard. Instead of taking the right path that God will bless, we take the easy path that ultimately leads to destruction. As you can gather from my stories, allowing myself to walk in destructive ways was not uncommon in my past life. Now I take my legacy seriously and will do anything to defend it and not allow anything

to tarnish it. This transition didn't happen overnight, but I can confidently say that I'm now on the right path to keeping that positive legacy intact.

When I think of an example of a Bible character who walked away from his legacy for a temporary fix, Esau comes to mind. In Genesis 25, the Bible tells a story of twin brothers, Esau and Jacob. Esau was born first and in all accounts was the alpha of the two, and Scripture described him as a redhead with his whole body being like a hairy garment. From birth, Jacob was second to his brother in stature: "The boys grew up, and Esau became a skillful hunter, a man of the open country, while Jacob was content to stay at home among the tents" (v. 27). I'm sure there was a growing resentment in Jacob for his brother's superiority, and that resentment took shape when he tricked Esau as he returned from a long hunting trip starving for food. Esau, famished, came home just as Jacob was cooking stew. "He said to Jacob, 'Quick, let me have some of that red stew! I'm famished!' … Jacob replied, 'First sell me your birthright.' 'Look, I am about to die,' Esau said. 'What good is the birthright to me?' But Jacob said, 'Swear to me first.' So he swore an oath to him, selling his birthright to Jacob. Then Jacob gave Esau some bread and some lentil stew. He ate and drank, and then got up and left. So, Esau despised his birthright" (vv. 30–34).

Esau wasn't about to die. He was hungry and made a permanent decision to a temporary problem. Because of his temporary desires, he traded his birthright and his legacy for a bowl of stew and was left with an empty bowl and an emptier heart.

We will all be hungry for something, but will we trade our birthrights as men of God, our legacies as warriors, for something less than greatness? I almost did when I settled for temporary healing in the wrong places, seeking to put Band-Aids on my ego

in lieu of seeking to be the man God created me to be. There is an unfair advantage for those who recognize the value and worth of their birthright in being a child of God and rising up to be the warriors he created them to be. For those who discover this truth, the advantage will come when you will never settle for less and will fight for that birthright to leave legacies in this world that are worth more than trading it all for a cup of stew.

If you are hungry today and impatient, do not settle to trade your birthright. Imagine the regret of Esau when he walked away from that meal because he also walked away from his legacy. There is not a bowl of stew, a sin, or anything in this world worth trading the very purpose and destiny God has for you.

I, for one, am grateful God is in the business of restoration and making old things new. And if, like me, you have made such a foolish trade in the past, it's not too late to recalibrate your life to the purpose God has for you. Humble yourself before God, repent to him and to others, and hand that bowl back to where it came from, reclaiming your mantle as a child of God, a warrior for the kingdom. This world needs you, and your feast is coming.

What a joy it is now to live a life fulfilled by God, who meets all my needs, heals all my hurts, and covers all my fears and anxieties. He is our unfair advantage and the only One who can fill a God-shaped hole and lead us to our destiny to leave a legacy in this world and beyond.

CHAPTER 10

NOT THE SOLUTION

Cast all your anxiety on him
because he cares for you.

1 PETER 5:7

I n a speech he made before the beginning of the war in Iraq, Saddam Hussein was quoted as saying, "Baghdad, its people and leadership, is determined to force the Mongols of our age to commit suicide at its gates."[11] Though he was wrong, unfortunately, he wasn't far off. Just look at the numbers: twenty-plus of our military warriors take their lives every single day.[12] If for no other reason, all combat veterans should hang on and fight through their own personal battles to prove this murderous dictator wrong. Thankfully for the world, this lunatic is now dead, but we must not allow him or our other enemies to claim and win the war over us and our families, even in their deaths. If we do, then we have willingly surrendered and handed them the final victory.

Our generation is not the first to suffer from the physical, mental, and spiritual tolls of war. We do not know for sure but can

be fairly certain that with the extensive combat experience of King David, he would have been wounded physically at some point in his life. However, throughout the book of Psalms, King David did not cry out about his physical wounds. Instead, in numerous passages this mighty warrior engaged in deep, fervent prayer with anguish in his words, as he cried out for God to restore and renew his soul. David faced trauma and struggled like other warriors before and after him, yet he had an unfair advantage in knowing where to find healing for the deepest wounds of his soul.

As in most situations in life, we can look to Jesus for the example. In the book of Mark, chapter 2, we see the amazing story of four friends who found out Jesus was in town and were determined to bring their paralyzed friend to him for healing. They did so despite the difficulty of moving a paralyzed guy confined to a mat from one point to another. I'm sure many of those reading this book have sadly had to carry a drunk friend or maybe move a limp body—not an easy task. I'm sure like many sick people, the man had a bad attitude and didn't want to see this Jesus, but what choice did he have when his friends carried him there?

When they got to the room Jesus was in, it was so packed they couldn't get through the door, but they didn't give up. They figured out a way to get him onto the roof, estimated where Jesus was, and then started tearing a hole in the roof; talk about persistence! This wasn't a cookie-cutter-home, suburban-American roof with plywood, tar paper, and shingles; this was a Middle Eastern roof made from thick mud and sticks. Can you imagine the scene? Jesus speaking in a packed house when, all of a sudden, the roof cracks open and parts of the ceiling start to rain down on him. I can't imagine because I get distracted when I'm speaking and a baby starts crying, let alone if someone was tearing a hole in the roof. This wasn't a small hole either because

the men made it big enough to stuff their paralyzed friend through and lower him down to Jesus.

As they lowered the man before Jesus, most of us would have assumed the same thing his friends did: that the paralyzed man's greatest need was to be healed of his physical ailment so he could walk again. Jesus demonstrated something completely different and significant here. He told the man, "Son, your sins are forgiven" (Mark 2:5). Jesus *did* heal the man physically but not before he demonstrated the initial healing of the deepest wound, healing the man's soul. In my own experience and my work with others who have experienced great despair, I have learned that you can tend to the body and the mind, but until you heal a man's soul, he will never fully be well. Jesus knew this and brilliantly demonstrated it. Yet many of us overlook the wounding of our souls and assume physical injuries are more serious. I had my share of physical injuries from my time in the military: a blown-out eardrum, broken vertebrate in my neck and back, and a variety of other scars to boast. My back and neck were probably the worst of them.

The first time I broke my back was in the '90s on a Joint Task Force-6 counternarcotics mission during a nighttime patrol as my team was searching for narcotics caches and underground grows for marijuana. I was the point man on a six-man patrol. It was a hot summer, and the vegetation was so thick that the poison oak vines were unavoidable; we had to crawl and tear our way through them to get from point A to point B. If you've been in a brush-infested valley in the cold, then you understand how the humidity from the vegetation, combined with the dampness, lowers the temperature by ten degrees. Just the same, the valleys we worked in for this thirty-day operation were ten degrees hotter and marred with 100 percent humidity. It was a nasty environment. The combination of the heat and the thick vegetation did

not aid tactical movement, so all movement had to take place at night. The easiest routes were the streambeds. One night, while on point, I made a nearly fatal error.

With my inexperience and lack of ambient light, I was struggling with the depth perception of my NOD (night observation device), so I took it off to try to go on my night vision. As I was leading the patrol through the streambed, struggling to see, I could hear the water flow of the stream increase. What I didn't know was that my next step would reveal a waterfall. As I stepped over the edge, the weight of my heavy rucksack immediately turned me upside down. I didn't have my waist strap buckled on my ruck, so it pulled me by my shoulders and exposed my lower back. After falling about fifteen feet in the dark, I landed on the streambed floor below. It was a bed of the finest assortment of large boulders, and my lower back found a big one. I had the wind knocked out of me, and it seemed forever before my teammates made their way down the banks and through the vegetation to reach me. After getting my breath, I couldn't stand up. I remember being really embarrassed for making such a goofball mistake and taking everyone off the mission. I would later learn that recon marines and big rucks sacks fall, often. But, at that time, my pride was hurt, and my legs weren't working.

After about an hour of trying to establish communications, my team was able to call in for a MedEvac (medical evacuation). After a prescription of Naprosyn, muscle relaxers, and a back brace for the two fractured lower vertebrates, I needed just six weeks of rest to be fit for duty again. I was young and durable back then.

My second back injury was during another inglorious moment of *idiocy*—only this time not on my part. (Why couldn't my story be just a little cooler than people doing stupid stuff and

me getting hurt?) Dave and I were relieving two teammates in Afghanistan, and we were riding in the open bed of a Toyota Hilux pickup truck. The guy driving (to protect his identity, let's just call him Captain Bonehead) was being a bonehead and driving down a high mountain road off of the well-known Khyber Pass like World Champion Off-Road Racer Danny Beauchamp. Captain Bonehead then suddenly hit—yes, another boulder. *What is it with me and boulders?* I was sitting flat on my butt and launched about fifty feet in the air!

Okay, that is the story I told my kids, and they believed it. Honestly, I don't know how high I went up; I just know that I landed flat on my butt and felt a crunch in my lower back. The compression shot all the way up my lower back to my neck. It hurt, and I was ticked. We were on a long road with no exits for several hours, so Dave and I decided to do what good Americans overseas do: commandeer a ride with the strangers in the vehicle behind us. Thankfully, they obliged. Captain Bonehead thought we were joking, but we stuck to our bitterness and refused to ride with him. We were enjoying the company of our new friends. There would be no MedEvac this time. I spent the next few months sucking it up before ever going to a doctor, and I later learned that I had shattered two vertebrae in my lower back and two in my neck. At this time in my life, I was no longer young and durable, and I still curse Captain Bonehead to this day.

My neck and back remain a constant reminder of my physical injuries, but I work around them and continue on with life. Yet no physical injury has ever knocked me down like the atomic bomb that exploded in my soul. Mark, an interpreter and companion of Peter, wrote, "What good is it for someone to gain the whole world, yet forfeit their soul?" (Mark 8:36). Even though I found so much success beyond my difficult circumstances, I still

found myself at a point of such despair; I was broken, scared, and hopeless about what the next moment would hold.

Initially, I thought mine was a mental problem. My level of intensity to do my job, my hatred for the enemy, and my anger started to turn into anxiety. When the physiological symptoms set in, I noticed my arms and the cheeks of my face would go numb, and I felt as if my throat were swelling shut. There were moments when I felt my heart was going to stop beating. At each incident, I thought I was having a heart attack. Other times, I felt out of body and started having lapses in memory. I was fearful and ashamed to tell anyone on my team because I thought they would think I was weak, and I knew I'd be pulled from my job.

I shoved it way down and tried to push through it. Even though I'm not a drinker, there were a few occasions when I tried to drink whiskey to numb it. That only made it worse. I thought I was going insane. It was during an operation, when I was working alone with local nationals, that I realized how foggy my mind had become; I couldn't recall much of the prior two weeks. In a brief moment of clarity, I realized I had made decisions that put me in danger, and I finally had to speak up. A short time later, I was back in the States sitting across from a clinical psychologist who told me the news of my PTSD diagnosis. That was devastating, and I felt as if I had lost everything. The shame of failure overtook me and sent me on a three-year downward spiral leading to Kathy and me facing a terrible divorce and my own battle with suicidal thoughts.

We sold our home, and I moved, alone, into an apartment. Over the previous years, I desperately needed someone to blame for the state I was in. Certainly, none of this could have been my fault. If my dad had been there for me as a boy and young man; if my mom had chosen me over my stepdad; if my brother had not been murdered when I was fourteen; if my task force in Afghanistan

had done things differently; if my wife had understood what I was going through; if all these people had done things differently, then maybe I wouldn't be in the mess I was in. That was the moment when I realized *it was me.*

It was such a clear revelation, and it hit me like a freight train. The reality of the choices I had made and the wake of destruction I had left behind overwhelmed me with guilt. All at once, I realized I had no one to blame for the position I was in. Even worse, at that moment, I realized how many people I had dragged down with me. The thought that I was such a hardship to my family brought me to the conclusion that taking my own life might be the best thing for them. For a two-week period, I tried to muster the will as I sat in my closet on multiple occasions with my loaded Glock 22 .40-caliber pistol in hand. I had believed my family would be sad with me gone but much better off. This terrifying reality, unfortunately, finds a home in the hopeless hearts of twenty-plus veterans per day.

It is horrifying to think I almost became one of those statistics and would have left my children with that legacy. However, I had heard that one in three children who loses a parent to suicide kills him- or herself as well. Knowing how much my children looked up to me was just enough motivation to pull me through the darkness of those distorted rationalizations. That thought allowed me to delay my demise as I contemplated how I could make my death look like an accident.

A short time later, Kathy came to my apartment and asked me a question that would not only change my life but also have a ripple effect on the lives of many others. She asked me how I could do all the things I had done in the military, in Afghanistan, and as an MMA fighter, but when it came to my family, I would quit. *Ouch*. No one had called me a quitter in my entire life, and it stung.

Yet, she was absolutely right. While I had found success in the professional areas in my life, when it came to the things that mattered most, I had quit. I quit on being a husband, a father, and on that young seventeen-year-old kid who raised his right hand and said he wanted to do something important with his life. I had quit on my own health and desire to live, and she called me out on it.

I had to make a decision. As crazy as it may sound, just like that, I decided I wanted to live again. I recognized I had a fight to win, and it was time for me to get back in it. I didn't yet know how to do it, but I was committed. With the help of others, a restoration of my faith, and finding a new purpose, I finally found myself on the other side.

With twenty-plus veteran suicides every day (that is nearly one death every hour), unfortunately, this isn't every warrior's story. After reaching a point of such hopelessness, these heroes make a permanent decision to a temporary problem. Twenty-plus of them a day; seventy-three hundred a year! In Vietnam, nearly sixty thousand Americans died, but the number we don't hear is that one hundred and sixty thousand Vietnam veterans committed suicide. Three times the number of veterans died by their own hands than at the hands of the enemy.

One of the more difficult things I've done at Mighty Oaks is speak to the spouses and parents of warriors who have taken their own lives. One profound example is Heather, the wife of a marine named Pete. Pete and Heather heard me speak at a church in Oklahoma when I offered to have veterans come to our program. Heather immediately recommended Pete come, but he said that other guys needed it more than he did. Only six months later, Pete stood in the back of a pickup truck surrounded by police as he held a pistol to his head. His final words were, "Tell my wife I love her and I'm doing this for her." He then pulled the trigger. I remem-

ber when Pastor Ron Woods of Pete and Heather's church called to tell me the news. If only he'd have given us a chance to help.

That bullet didn't kill Pete; his pride and unwillingness to get the help he needed killed him. Heather was devastated, but a few months later, she asked Kathy and me to start sharing her side of the story with other veterans. She wanted to challenge other veterans so they would know the truth: Pete didn't make her life better; he devastated the lives of those who loved him that day. She shares the story of Pete's legacy, the mess he left behind, the hurt and pain, how his parents will never be the same, and the nights when she needs her husband and he isn't there. She talks about her final moments with Pete, as he was laid out on a metal table, and she had her head on his chest listening for his heart to beat but hearing nothing.

One of the things Heather said to me that I will never forget is, "Suicide doesn't get rid of your pain; it just transfers it to those you love." She is one of the bravest human beings I have ever met. I've seen her stand in front of hundreds of spiritually broken warriors and literally save their lives by telling her and Pete's story. When I hear her speak, I look at her and think, *Never will my wife stand up in front of other warriors, weeping and telling a tale of me quitting.* For me, the thought of leaving such a tragic legacy became a catalyst for change. I wanted my life to mean something. I wanted to leave a legacy worth passing down. We are all leaving a legacy one way or another, and yours can be a great one, a name for others to remember. Don't end it with an exclamation point of failure, and don't leave a wake of destruction for others. Why should we finish the job the enemy couldn't?

The Old Testament story of Job is a story most of us can relate to. Job had everything. He was a wealthy man with a large family who loved and respected him. He had a great reputation and

a large circle of friends. But, in a moment, everything changed. For reasons that he would never understand, he lost everything. His children were killed, he lost his good health, and his friends began to accuse him of doing something to anger God. If all that was not enough, at the absolute lowest point in his life, his wife advised him to give up. Her exact words were, "Curse God and die!" (Job 2:9). When Job hit his rock bottom and didn't know what to do, the one person in his life who should have supported him told him to take his own life. Maybe you cannot relate to the depth of such great loss experienced by Job. However, the feeling of complete loss and hopelessness is something most of us will experience in our lives. Maybe, during moments like this, you resonate with the advice given by Job's wife to simply end it all.

Thankfully, Job didn't take his wife's faulty guidance but rather provided an example for us all as we face moments of despair. Job had an unfair advantage in understanding that life wasn't about him but about God and serving others. Job recognized that life is a combination of both good and bad things, and we need to trust God regardless of what is happening around us. He responded to his wife: "'You are talking like a foolish woman. Shall we accept good from God, and not trouble?' In all this, Job did not sin in what he said" (v. 10).

There is always a brighter day, but sometimes there is darkness before the light, or as USMC Medal of Honor recipient Corporal Kyle Carpenter, who selflessly threw his body onto a Taliban hand grenade to save his friend, said, "Out of the darkest of times we have had, have come some of the greatest things."[13] Never give up!

CHAPTER 11

WHO'S IN YOUR CORNER?

A friend loves at all times,
and a brother is born for a time of adversity.

PROVERBS 17:17

When I fought for *The Legacy* Fighting Championship Inaugural Bantamweight World Title belt, thousands of fans packed the sold-out, historic Houston, Texas, Arena Theater. I wasn't only living in the Houston area at the time but also owned one of the largest Brazilian jiu-jitsu/mixed martial arts schools in Texas, so I had hundreds of teammates, students, and local support there to cheer me on. When you're the main event on a fight card, you have a long wait until the end of the event for your turn, and your closest coaches and training partners share your locker room. There are moments of joking and having fun, moments of talking, strategy, and drilling technique, and moments of eerie silence. As each fight ends, you become more aware of the ticking of the clock as your time nears. Every time you hear the crowd roar for a finish, you're reminded that time *isn't* stopping, and

your moment is fast approaching. It's an emotional roller coaster of excitement and anxiety building up to one climatic moment. I've always loved this part of fighting; it offers a true self-evaluation of what you're mentally made of. These times always brought me closer to God, even when my faith was weak.

Because I was the hometown fighter, my opponent walked out first. Moments later, it would be my turn to take the walk. When the State Athletic Commission coordinator led me out the doors from the backstage locker room, I was overwhelmed by what I heard and saw. The local Houston crowd at the arena went crazy, standing up and cheering their support. I'm sure many cheered against me, too, but in that moment, it seemed like every single person in the place was cheering for me to step into that cage. It was so overwhelming that I went from my focused fight mode to being emotionally touched as I felt tears well up.

My boxing coach, Lewis Wood, a.k.a. the General, noticed my emotion and wasn't too happy. He was a stern, no-fluff coach, which is how he earned his nickname. He had been there before as a 33-1 pro boxer, having fought all over the world and coached many boxing, MMA, and UFC greats. The General grabbed me, shook me, and sternly said, "Hey, look at me, don't pay attention to any of that s—t. Focus on what you came here to do!" I snapped back into fight mode and made the walk to the cage to face my undefeated opponent. Neither of us had ever been beaten in professional competition, but that would soon change for one of us; *it wouldn't be me.*

As in most of my fights, I can remember every detail, down to the Vaseline being wiped onto my eyebrows and the bridge of my nose. I remember my cornerman placing my mouthpiece in my mouth, and I knew it was time. I walked into the cage, and the door shut behind me. It was my opponent and me, alone,

with only a referee to guide the action that would soon take place between us. When the referee said "Fight!" I circled left and met my opponent in the center of the cage as we both teed off on each other with punches. One minute and forty-six seconds into the action, I secured a textbook rear-naked choke to become the first *Legacy FC* Bantamweight Champion. Moments later, the LFC president and now UFC matchmaker, Mick Maynard, would strap the championship title belt around my waist. It was an incredible feeling of pride in representing my team for such an achievement.

Through so many fights in my life, inside and outside the cage, there have been those who have cheered for me and others who cheered against me, yet the General's words always hold true: "Don't pay attention to any of that s—t. Focus on what you came here to do!" *Win*. You will always have those who stand for you and those who stand against you, but there will come a moment when the clock ticks to your time, and you need to be able to step up to the battle line and fight. When those moments come, pay no attention to the background and have the right people in your corner who will tell you the words you *need* to hear, not what you *want* to hear; there is a big difference.

Sadly, while I seemed to always have the right men in my corner to win the toughest fights in the cage and the most incredible teammates in the military, that wasn't always the case in my personal life. When Kathy called me out as a quitter and I felt the desire rise up to face her challenge and get back into the fight, my intuition told me I wouldn't be able to do it alone. An inventory of my life brought the sad realization that even though I had a thousand or more "friends" in my circle, I had no one who I could trust to hold me accountable, only people who would tell me what I wanted to hear, not what I needed to hear. What a pathetic place to be—and I had systematically put myself there.

Humbly, I asked Kathy to help me find a man who could hold me accountable, and God brought a man named Steve Toth into my life. I love the King James Version of the beloved Proverb 27:17, "Iron sharpeneth iron; so a man sharpeneth the countenance of his friend." Steve was the iron I needed to sharpen me. He would not only become my mentor but also my accountability partner, my friend, and an example of what an authentic man of God and a true brother looked like.

I first met with Steve at a Starbucks. I had essentially written a military-style "5-Paragraph Order" (terminology for military operations plan) of how I was going to fix my life. I had all the right things ready to say to this man and knew I had the gift of manipulating people and situations. I thought that this would be easy, but God had other plans, and my games didn't work with Steve. You see, Steve's greatest gift, at least for this situation, was his extreme ADD (attention-deficit disorder). Well, in reality, a doctor may not have diagnosed his ADD, but it is certainly a big part of his personality. He simply didn't have the time or the patience to deal with my game or attempts to say all the right things. When I slid my fixing-my-life operations plan in front of him, he glanced at it and slid it right back to me, firmly saying, "You're likely going to end up right back where you are now!" He didn't even look at my plan, and, believe me, it was a great one.

"Why?" I asked. "It's a good plan!"

Steve boldly said, "If it doesn't include God, you will fail and fall right back on your face again. If you won't do it with God, I can't help you."

What I didn't know was that the last time Steve had mentored a man, he did so without such authority; instead, he was a bit more timid in his approach. He didn't tell the man the hard truths, and that man had taken his own life only months before we

met. Steve wasn't going to make that mistake again, and he told me exactly what I *needed* to hear.

In our work at Mighty Oaks, we have tokened a challenging question for the warriors who attend: *If what you're doing isn't working, then why not try something different?* It's the same question I had to ask myself. The truth is that nothing I had tried before worked. Not medication, counseling, or even Brazilian jiu-jitsu and mixed martial arts. It was time for me to try something different, and for the first time in my life, I truly gave God a chance and completely surrendered to him.

For a year afterward, Steve mentored me in biblical manhood, and what I discovered along the way was incredible. I had believed the lie that I had to choose between a life of faith and a life as a warrior. I couldn't have been more wrong. The Scriptures revealed the man that God created and intended me to be. In fact, it was the type of man and warrior I had always desired to be. I was hooked, and the more I tried to calibrate my life to this biblical model of manhood, the more I found restoration in my life and my family, and things started to change.

I realized that while I still could remember the past, it no longer defined me. Don't get me wrong, I still got angry, but I had control over how I reacted. I came to the realization that the circumstances of my past had not led me to rock bottom, but the choices I had made led me there. I never lost control of the ability to choose differently. Now I understood a model in which to make the right choices: God's model. There was a clear moment for me when I truly found the cure for what I had faced, for PTSD or life's hardships in general. Everything else had failed—the pills, counseling, Brazilian jiu-jitsu, and MMA—but when I simply made the choice to align my life to the life God created me to live, I found hope, healing, and the thing we all need most: *purpose.*

There is an old saying commonly credited to Mark Twain: "The two most important days in your life are the day you are born and the day you find out why." I believe the path Steve led me on—to align my life with the life God created me to live—revealed my very purpose. I will be forever indebted to Steve for such a gift, but at the core of that new purpose was the compulsion to share it, to pay it forward. Like I said, I felt like I had now found the cure. It felt as if I had stage-four terminal cancer and were dying, but Steve stepped in and introduced me to the antidote. I had to share it with others, and Mighty Oaks Warrior Programs was birthed as a result of that. Steve's mentoring was the foundation that challenged me to reach other warriors struggling just as I did. From the gratitude that was now deep within my heart, I had an obligation to pay it forward—to pay forward the challenge Kathy gave me, the mentorship Steve gave me, and the news of a second chance that God gives us all. Through our work at Mighty Oaks, we have been blessed to bring that message to thousands of warriors around the country and, to date, have had more than fifteen hundred warriors graduate our core one-week Legacy Program.

I have a good friend who always says, "Show me your friends and I'll show you your future." The Bible says it like this: "Do not be misled: 'Bad company corrupts good character'" (1 Corinthians 15:33). Still today when I look at Steve, I know I'm in good company, and I see a future that I am now honored to step into. Steve is the model for brotherhood I now strive to be for others and whom I surround myself with. Men who will tell one another what they *need to hear*, not what they *want to hear*. Through Mighty Oaks, God has brought such amazing men into my life to not do this work alone. He has even brought me a very best friend, who challenges me like Kathy did and invests in me like Steve did; in fact, you will hear from Jeremy Stalnecker in the

afterword of this book. Jeremy and these other men in my life are true friends who I can trust with my deepest and darkest secrets, fears, and struggles ... without judgment but with accountability and correction. I'm now bonded with a brotherhood of like-minded men, equally yoked and pursuing a righteous life of character, integrity, and honor. In knowing God has an important mission and purpose for me in this world, I am grateful I am not called to do this life alone.

As much as I'd like to write an entire book about the brotherhood between Jesus and his disciples, I'll save it for another day. They were indeed a renegade crew on a mission to rescue humanity and stand against the evil and institutionalized religious hypocrisy of the day. Yet, I'd like to talk about the bond between two *friends* ... two *warriors*: David, the giant-slayer and the future king of Israel, and Jonathan, the brave prince who climbed the side of a cliff with his armor bearer to sneak into the enemy barracks and start a fight when everyone else lacked the courage.

In 1 Samuel 18:1, the Bible described their bond as brothers. "Jonathan became one in spirit with David, and he loved him as himself." Since the Scriptures talk so much about the intimacy of these two men's relationship, let's be clear. These men were not weak; these were battle-hardened warriors. David entered the scene of Scripture as the boy who stood against and killed the giant, Goliath. From there you can follow the story of David through his life as a warrior in numerous battles. A beast on the battlefield, he eventually became the God-appointed and beloved king of Israel. Through many highs and lows, he had a friend named Jonathan. Jonathan was heir to the throne and was willing to step aside for David to be king. *Why?* Because the two of them shared a pursuit for the things of God. Jonathan believed that God was raising David up to be the next king of Israel and that he

would replace Jonathan's father, even though Jonathan was next in line for the throne.

"And Jonathan made a covenant with David because he loved him as himself. Jonathan took off the robe he was wearing and gave it to David, along with his tunic, and even his sword, his bow and his belt" (vv. 3–4). These men exemplify everything masculine, yet they had a deep and passionate love for each other; it was authentic, real, selfless, and built on like-mindedness as they both put God first in their lives. Jonathan gave his friend his robe, his armor, and his sword and bow. You must understand the significance here. His robe identified him as royalty as the prince. He unselfishly relinquished his status for his friend. He gave him his armor, which protected him, his sword that he used to defend himself, and his bow that he used to hunt and provide for himself. While heir to the throne, the presumed future king of Israel, Jonathan gave his friend David everything he had, including humbly stepping aside to see God's will fulfilled with David as king, even though David had been raised as a shepherd boy.

In one of the most intimate scenes of friendship in the Bible, we see the depth of loyalty and love among brothers—the same intimacy lived by many military warriors—as a friend loses his brother in battle. David cried out, "How the mighty have fallen in battle! Jonathan lies slain on your heights. I grieve for you, Jonathan my brother; you were very dear to me. Your love for me was wonderful, more wonderful than that of women. How the mighty have fallen! The weapons of war have perished!" (2 Samuel 1:25–27). More wonderful than that of women? Don't get it twisted. We all know that the love among true brothers is rare and special, especially those intimate bonds forged on the fields of battle. In the book *Tender Warrior*, author Stu Weber, a US Army Special Force's Green Beret and Vietnam veteran, clarified this moment perfectly:

A war-hardened veteran penned these words after his best buddy fell in battle. They were written by a warrior, with the piercing grief only a soldier mourning for a comrade-in-arms could begin to understand. Twisted words? No. These are words straight and true—a swift, clean arrow shot from the heart of scripture. David wrote these words after the death of his friend Jonathan on the bloody slopes of Mount Gilboa. What the son of Jesse expressed without shame in that lament was something that has burned deep in the soul of every man in one way or another for generations beyond memory. A desire for friendship, man to man. A desire for friendship with nothing between. A yearning for friendship so real, so strong, so compelling, it is willing to share everything about itself and make deep and powerful promises.[14]

Beyond the tears of heartbreak about losing his best friend on the battlefield at Mount Gilboa, David was no doubt a warrior. But the same guy who slaughtered and cut off the foreskins of two-hundred enemy soldiers to win the princess's hand in marriage was also a real-life normal man, not a fictional Bible character. Like most of us, David was a man who bled, cried, and struggled. Beyond the accolades, the tales of his life include struggles with pride, anxiety, women, and even doubt. However, through it all, David had an unfair advantage in the trials and tribulations he faced; he had a true brother to lean on, and his name was Jonathan.

Who's in your corner when you step into the arena of combat? Is it someone you can count on? Does he or she have a like-minded pursuit for the things of God as David and Jonathan

shared? Will he or she lead and inspire you like Steve Toth did for me when I needed a cornerman for the greatest fight of my life?

We were created to have community, to have brotherhood. You cannot be who God created you to be and do what he calls you to do alone. You were never meant to. If you don't have the kind of relationship, the kind of brotherhood, that David found in Jonathan, that I found in Steve and others along the way since, *then you need to desperately seek it out.* Imagine you were drowning and needed air. How desperate and focused would you be to fight for just one breath? That's the level of urgency and focus you must have to make godly and authentic brotherhood a priority in your life. When you have such brothers to lock arms with, you will truly have an unfair advantage and win the battles ahead.

CHAPTER 12

A PRE-DECISION TO WIN

Give me six hours to chop down a tree
and I will spend the first four sharpening the axe.

ABRAHAM LINCOLN

As a warrior and a fighter, you have to know you're in a fight, learn about your opponent, his strategies and weaknesses, decide when and when not to engage, and most of all, make the pre-decision to win. This is the same for any fight worth fighting in your life. Whether it is on the battlefield or to claim your place as a great husband, father, or friend, to achieve a goal or overcome any shortfall in your life, you need to have a willingness to fight. You won't always know what to do, but know now that you will have to do something. President Theodore Roosevelt once said, "In any moment of decision, the best thing you can do is the right thing, the next best thing is the wrong thing, and the worst thing you can do is nothing."[15] You will have to decide the battle is worth the victory and make a pre-decision that you are going to do something—and you are going to win. Any time you decide it is

time to fight, you better decide to win. Fighting hard doesn't mean simply trying; it means fight as if you were the third monkey on the ramp of Noah's Ark…and *it's starting to rain*. Be diligent and ferocious!

As I travel around the country to speak, I often get to meet with teenage boys aspiring to become a Navy SEAL, Green Beret, or Recon Marine. They all ask the same question: "What do I need to do to prepare for the training?" I can give the obvious answers: "Get in shape…run, swim, get strong…eat well," and I do, but I also tell them what everyone needs to hear before they face a worthy challenge: "Make a pre-decision to finish!" Simple, right? Decide in advance. Why? Because any fight worth winning, any challenge worth achieving, will get hard, and when it does, most people quit. I ask these aspiring future special operators, "What will you do when you have cellulitis between your thighs where the sand rubbed your legs raw? When you have bronchitis-filled lungs; when your IT bands in your knees hurt so bad that you feel like you can't walk one more step; when the forty-degree water tells your mind that recruiting poster doesn't look so sexy anymore, and you have one hundred possible legitimate excuses to justify quitting…what will you do?" The answer better be, "I will do what I came here to do: finish!" That is how you win a fight and accomplish any challenge in life; you make a pre-decision to win and do so despite all opposition.

Preparation is everything. As noted above, President Lincoln is said to have remarked, "Give me six hours to chop down a tree and I will spend the first four sharpening the axe." In the Marines, my instructors taught me to prepare for things in advance using the seven P's: Proper Prior Planning Prevents Piss Poor Performance. Seasoned warfighters make decisions for every possible thing to go wrong in advance. You don't patrol out of a FOB (for-

ward operating base) and wait until you make contact with the enemy in a "contact right" scenario, then call a time out, rally up, and decide what to do. No, you decide in advance; you make a pre-decision on what you will do when you face the enemy so you will react correctly, perform under the pressure of battle, and win. So, why can't we do that in life? Make a pre-decision of what you will do when you face life's challenges so that when you face the ambushes Satan has for you, you will react correctly, perform, and win. The truth is you can. When you start forward thinking the battles ahead, studying your enemy, and anticipating his attacks, you can plan and strategize in advance to be prepared and have an unfair advantage in the battles we all face in this world.

As a professional MMA fighter, I've had the privilege of training with some of the world's best athletes and coaches. For two of my fight-training camps I had the honor to work with Randy Couture and one of his long-time wrestling partners Brad Anderson, an Olympic Greco wrestling team alternate. These two guys are amazing examples of men of grit and a warrior's spirit. Most everyone knows Randy as "The Natural," six-time UFC champion, Hall of Famer, and one of the sport's corner-stones. If you don't know him as an athlete, you may remember his roles in many action films, such as *The Expendables*.

What many don't know is that Randy is incredibly kind and a man of high character who is always down-to-earth and, at the same time, has the natural ability to pass those traits on to others through his coaching. Randy is a strategist and adamant about training camps and competition for fight day. One day during training, he challenged me to "visualize the win." I have heard this all my life in martial arts. However, Randy had a contagious passion about it, and I knew he had something valuable to share, so I listened and took it all in.

After one of Brad's grueling torture/training sessions for my upcoming fight against UFC fighter Joseph Sandoval, Randy ran me through a visualization training session. As I lay on the mats, drenched in sweat and still catching my breath from two hours of work, Randy's voice led me into the future as he challenged me to imagine it was the night of the fight. He took my mind on a visual journey, starting in my locker room as I warmed up to the "minutes out" cue from the event coordinator. I walked out to the music I had selected for my entry to the cage: Johnny Cash's "Ain't No Grave."

Randy's voice continued, "The crowd is cheering and everyone's watching." He continued to describe every detail from walking to the cage to the inspection to the cage door shutting. It was Sandoval and I alone, with only a referee to guide the action. When the referee said "Fight!" I circled left to the southpaw's right side like I had trained hundreds of times. It felt so real in my mind, all the details we had worked on in training. I visualized my strengths and Sandoval's weaknesses. In a moment, I had walked through my opponent. Randy's voice even took me to the moment when I raised my hands in victory.

One month later, there I stood, face-to-face with Sandoval. The visualization was real life now. Amazingly, it would all play out exactly how we had spoken it, seen it, and claimed it—even through the moment where I raised my hands in victory. I consider it a truly incredible night in my career as a fighter, but as a man who has faced struggles and witnessed the struggles of others, Randy taught me a valuable lesson: If you're going to get in a fight, know your opponent, visualize your victory and claim it—all the way through the moment when your hands are raised in victory. Don't let anything stop you!

An unfair advantage that I believe I had in the Sandoval fight was not just my visualization training through Randy, but at that

point in my life, I was also solidified in my walk and faith with God. One of the main reasons I was fighting was that HD Net agreed to feature a special segment on my work at Mighty Oaks Foundation and broadcast a message for other veterans who might need help. I don't believe God is in the business of caring who wins or loses MMA fights, but I do believe God cares about the little things that bring us joy. He honors those who honor him, as we give him glory in our victories and even in our defeats. Trusting his will for my life alleviated the constant pressure of winning that previously over-whelmed me when I competed. I never had a fear of fighting but of failing. As I leaned on him and spent much time in prayer, I was able to simply train, have fun, and enjoy competing, while knowing God was in control.

Cutting weight for the Sandoval fight was insane. I went from 155 pounds to 125 pounds in seven weeks to make weight and walked in the cage the next day already back up to 153 pounds. During the weight cut, I remember being in the sauna, struggling to remain in the heat despite the dehydration every second. If you don't focus, a panic can come over you to survive. Your body literally feels like it is dying. Few things in life are more miserable than cutting weight for a fight. I had music playing in the sauna and kept it on repeat for the Casting Crowns' song "Praise You in This Storm." The lyrics come directly from Psalm 121 in the Bible: "I lift my eyes unto the hills. Where does my help come from? My help comes from the Lord, the Maker of Heaven and Earth." If God made the hills, heaven, earth, and even Joseph Sandoval, then he could definitely give me favor to win this fight, but did he care about the results? At that time, I didn't know.

Either way, it didn't stop me from trusting his will, and I had made the pre-decision to glorify him in victory or defeat. I had also made a pre-decision to win. I told my Muay Thai kickboxing coach

and USMF Thai boxing champion, Daniel Kim, who is a fellow Christian, that I was fighting for the microphone. The winner gets the mic on a televised fight, and I had a message to give everyone listening about what God was doing at Mighty Oaks; that was my goal. Too bad for Sandoval who was in the way because after only fifty-one seconds of the first round, I had choked him out and was standing center cage with MMA sports commentator, former UFC Champion, and Hall of Famer Pat Miletich doing exactly what I went there to do: win, share the message of Mighty Oaks, and give glory to the One who made it all possible. As a warrior and a fighter, you can do so many great things to plan and prepare for a fight, but the best thing you can do is to intentionally align your will with his. We all should glorify God in everything we do, even a sporting event.

Sometimes God will even put us in what seems to be a no-win situation when we are trying to point the credit to him. Why? So he alone will get the credit and *not us*. Such has been the case for Mighty Oaks Foundation, where we have found extreme favor and success that has way more to do with God than with us. People often ask me, "How has Mighty Oaks been so successful so quickly?" The truth is I cannot point to anything other than God's favor. We started with nothing, against all odds and much opposition, yet the organization is thriving and doing incredible work. We can only point to God's provisions for this to have happened.

What God has done for Mighty Oaks, he also displayed in a crazy battle in the book of Judges. After the Israelites entered the promised land, a tribe called the Midianites heavily oppressed them. They would pillage their homesteads, destroy their crops, and kill their livestock. The people began hiding, living in caves; some even turned away from worshiping God. At times when

there is such oppression, God will always look to warriors to stand up and fight and see his plan through.

In this case, God called on Gideon. The odds were stacked against him from the beginning: he was the weakest member of his family, and he was from Manasseh, the weakest Israelite tribe—and Gideon let the Lord know it:

> When the angel of the Lord appeared to Gideon, he said, "The Lord is with you, mighty warrior." "Pardon me, my lord," Gideon replied, "but if the Lord is with us, why has all this happened to us? Where are all his wonders that our ancestors told us about when they said, 'Did not the Lord bring us up out of Egypt?' But now the Lord has abandoned us and given us into the hand of Midian." The Lord turned to him and said, "Go in the strength you have and save Israel out of Midian's hand. Am I not sending you?" "Pardon me, my lord," Gideon replied, "but how can I save Israel? My clan is the weakest in Manasseh, and I am the least in my family." The Lord answered, "I will be with you, and you will strike down all the Midianites, leaving none alive." (Judges 6:12–16)

Gideon literally argued with God! "Who? Me? I'm not your guy! I'm not strong enough!" Yet God said, "Am I not sending you? … I will be with you, and you will strike down all the Midianites, leaving none alive." God was using the unexpected to do the unimaginable.

Gideon decided to follow God's instructions, so he mustered an army of thirty-two thousand to go into battle against an estimated one hundred and thirty five thousand Midianite fighters. But God informed Gideon that he had gathered too many men. Whoa!

How can you have too many warriors when you're already outnumbered four to one? But God wanted the world to see and to know what would happen to any enemy who persecuted his people.

God told Gideon to send home any scared fighters, so twenty-two thousand of them left. Only ten thousand remained. Now they were outnumbered fourteen to one, but God told Gideon there were still too many. I can imagine what Gideon was thinking: *What in the world? God, you asked me to do this impossible thing. I already told you that I'm the least qualified. I raise the best force I can, and now I have to dismantle it?* Many mid-level military leaders have experienced the same frustration as they are forced to follow the lead of upper-echelon commanders who see the bigger picture. One thing that makes warriors successful is a willing obedience to follow orders and trust leadership. Gideon did.

God sent Gideon down to the river to select the final men who would fight and defeat the Midianites:

> There the Lord told him, "Separate those who lap the water with their tongues as a dog laps from those who kneel down to drink." Three hundred of them drank from cupped hands, lapping like dogs. All the rest got down on their knees to drink. The Lord said to Gideon, "With the three hundred men that lapped I will save you and give the Midianites into your hands. Let all the others go home." (Judges 7:5–7)

I've heard mixed views about why the three hundred were selected. All our views may be wrong, but I believe the men who drank from their cupped hands kept their eyes outward and on guard and showed an ability to be alert and capable, while the men who got on their knees put their face in the water and were not alert fighters.

Just Gideon and three hundred men remained, and that night God instructed Gideon to go to the Midian camp because the time had come when he would give the Midianites into Gideon's hands. But God knows our hearts and our fears—including Gideon's fear that he had only three hundred men to face the fighting force of one hundred and thirty-five thousand men that had ruled them for nearly a decade. The Bible says the enemy was so numerous that they were as thick as locusts, and they and their camels "could no more be counted than the sand on the seashore" (v. 12). Then God told Gideon, "If you are afraid to attack, go down to the camp with your servant Purah and listen to what they are saying. Afterward, you will be encouraged to attack the camp" (v. 10–11).

Gideon and Purah snuck into the camp and heard a man tell his friend, "'I had a dream,' he was saying. 'A round loaf of barley bread came tumbling into the Midianite camp. It struck the tent with such force that the tent overturned and collapsed.' His friend responded, 'This can be nothing other than the sword of Gideon son of Joash, the Israelite. God has given the Midianites and the whole camp into his hands'" (vv. 13–14).

Hearing this dream was just what Gideon needed. He knelt down and worshiped God for this, then went back to his three hundred men and said, "Get up! The Lord has given the Midianite camp into your hands" (v. 15).

Under the cover of night, the men approached the camp of their unsuspecting foes. When Gideon sounded the attack, the three hundred warriors surrounded the enemy camp with torches and trumpets, sounding the trumpets and shouting, "For the Lord and for Gideon!" (v. 18). The Midianites panicked and began to kill everyone they saw—which in the dark was their own army. Gideon and his men mopped up the remainder, including two Midianite kings whom Gideon himself killed.

Gideon had an unfair advantage because he trusted God even facing a seemingly impossible mission. Despite his initial doubts, Gideon's faith led him to a pre-decision to win going into the battle. We see his confidence increase and his advantage grow after cutting his army by 99 percent, from thirty-two thousand to three hundred. God made them understand that true victory comes from his hand.

When you go into a fight trusting that God is in control, you will have peace, confidence, and an unfair advantage over your adversary. And if you are still measuring victory based on whether you win or lose, the reality is that you cannot lose if you are doing what God wants you to do. The real victory is in knowing and believing this, and when you do, you will leave behind a legacy that others will be proud of and will want to follow.

CHAPTER 13

A TIME TO FIGHT

There is a time for everything,
and a season for every activity under the heavens:
a time to be born and a time to die…
a time to kill and a time to heal…
a time to weep and a time to laugh…
a time to love and a time to hate,
a time for war and a time for peace.

ECCLESIASTES 3:1–8

There is a time for everything in life, as is written in the book of Ecclesiastes by King Solomon, the son of the warrior-king David. Arguably one of the wisest men to ever live wrote this book about the wisdom he wanted to pass on to us after he was gone. His concluding words in the book are, "Now all has been heard; here is the conclusion of the matter: Fear God and keep his commandments, for this is the duty of all mankind. For God will bring every deed into judgment, including every hidden

thing, whether it is good or evil" (Ecclesiastes 12:13–14). King Solomon was known for his wisdom. He also knew that life had up and down seasons and there was a time and place for everything.

We, as men, often are impatient and lack wisdom in the area of discerning which battles are worth fighting and when to fight them. I certainly know this is the case with young military men, especially my fellow marines. I can remember so many times being part of, or witnessing, the most idiotic stuff, mostly out of a lack of direction and purpose or general boredom. One night, when I was much younger, I was living in the barracks in Twentynine Palms, California. Some of my recon teammates and I were enjoying a movie and beers. I honestly never was a beer drinker or big on any alcohol; however, I used to think it was pretty hysterical to watch what would happen when bored marines would get drunk in the barracks. Despite my present-day ministerial status, I will confess, at that time of my life, this really entertained me. This particular night would not disappoint as my drunken marine brothers would deliver.

My buddies Melton, Ohlson, Terrell, and I were watching a movie called *Point Break*, starring Keanu Reeves. Much to our surprise, Ohlson had invited a marine from another unit to join us that night. *Never a good idea!* You see, for those who haven't served, here is how it works: If there are services from multiple countries around, then the US military stands united. If it is only the US military, then there is surely service-to-service rivalry. If there are marine tankers and infantry around, there is a feud brewing. Heaven forbid if there are multiple infantry platoons in an armory cleaning weapons together because there will surely be a fistfight. Competition is so embedded in military personnel, especially marines, that there must be a rival, and that means someone will always be the odd man out.

This poor guy came into our barracks and somehow started an argument over who Keanu Reeves's wingman was. *Was it Nick Nolte or Gary Busey?* It was on when Terrell made it clear that the correct answer was Nick Nolte with a right cross to the poor guy's face. As Terrell and this guy were fighting, I was getting my dose of Friday night entertainment. All of a sudden, Melton decided to jump in by coming off the top rack of the bunks with a "Stone Cold" Steve Austin elbow to the head of the guy who said it was Busey. (It turns out, it really was Busey, but who cares?) You don't need a valid reason to "go WWE" during a good barracks fight. Fortunately, no marines were injured during the making of this story. I know Terrell and the other marine would fight side by side against a common enemy, but military guys love to fight, and thankfully, for the preservation of freedom, they are wired to do so. That doesn't mean that we should do so recklessly, for in every time and place there is "a time for war and a time for peace"—a time to fight and a time not to.

Here is a side note for transitioning military veterans: Military life is different than civilian life, and contrary to how normal this story may seem to you, this behavior would not be acceptable on a corporate business trip with your coworkers. *Just a note!*

The truth is that if we are going to be the men God calls us to be, we must be willing to fight, but at the same time, we need to have discernment over which battles to engage in and who we are fighting so we can make the best decisions, in advance, to win. We are all in a spiritual war against evil, a war against Satan himself. Peter warned us about our enemy, to "be alert and of sober mind. Your enemy the devil prowls around like a roaring lion looking for someone to devour" (1 Peter 5:8). If you want to win in warfare, you better know who you're fighting. Make no mistake, you are fighting an enemy who has deceived and defeated many

men before you. So, what will you do? Pretend you're not in a fight and that Satan is a figment of imagination? Do you see him as a villain from a fairy-tale storyline? If that is your view, you'll get hit anyway. The only difference is that you won't see it coming, and one day you'll look up and wonder why you're on your back, knocked down in life.

As I reflect on my own life to this point, I think back on how many pointless fights I engaged in, the time I wasted on pursuits for selfish gain, and the arguments I had that cost me relationships and opportunities. So many hills that I was willing to die on for pointless and unworthy causes, all the time overlooking this big picture about fighting for the most important things, the things God had in store for me. How much pain and wasted energy I would have saved myself and others if I only had turned to God for wisdom for the battles he called me to engage in and the understanding of when to fight and what is truly worth fighting for.

I believe much of the world today misunderstands Jesus as a pacifist who would shy away from conflict and turn the other cheek to his enemies. Nothing could be further from the truth. Jesus didn't shy from conflict. He met it head-on like a freight train with zero compromise in his mission on earth to boldly share the truth and reveal his plan for the world. In fact, his ministry was rooted in confrontation with the institution, the religious rule of the day, and he did so with boldness, courage, and, at times, heated passion. Jesus had an unfair advantage by knowing there were times to dig in and fight and times to stand down. He is the example we must follow in knowing there is a time to fight the battles right in front of us and a time to be patient and wait for the opportunity to fight the bigger battles so that we will win the war.

The apostle Peter, however, didn't always know when to fight and what battles were worthwhile. He had moments of

courage and moments he cowered down. Yet he had an unfair advantage of hearing Jesus as he guided him to understand the battle he was in. Before the Last Supper, we see Peter's desire to fight and defend Jesus after he told Peter and the disciples that he would be arrested and killed. The Bible says, "Peter took him aside and began to rebuke him. 'Never, Lord!' he said. 'This shall never happen to you!' Jesus turned and said to Peter, 'Get behind me, Satan! You are a stumbling block to me; you do not have in mind the concerns of God, but merely human concerns'" (Matthew 16:22–23). Jesus had a plan, but Peter, because of his ignorance, didn't understand where and when to fight.

Later, during the Last Supper, Jesus spoke to his disciples about the days to come. Jesus knew that while his sacrifice on the cross would create a way to save mankind from sin and death, it wouldn't end the hardships of this world for those who believed in him. It would only get worse. His last words at the supper were, "'But now if you have a purse, take it, and also a bag; and if you don't have a sword, sell your cloak and buy one.' … The disciples said, 'See, Lord, here are two swords.' 'That's enough!' he replied" (Luke 22:36–38). He knew his disciples would face a dangerous time and many enemies and have to fight to continue his mission.

The next day, when they came to arrest Jesus, Peter drew his sword and struck the servant of the high priest, cutting off his ear. Jesus stopped him and said, "Do you think I cannot call on my Father, and he will at once put at my disposal more than twelve legions of angels? But how then would the Scriptures be fulfilled that say it must happen in this way?" (Matthew 26:53–54). Jesus told Peter to put down the sword he wielded to protect him, which was likely one of the two swords referred to at the Last Supper.

Jesus knew a bigger battle was coming and a war to be won. That war was not going to be won that day in the garden with the

priests and soldiers, but he had to remind Peter of that, and while he was brokenhearted and scared, Peter listened. He had an unfair advantage in hearing Jesus' voice and instruction that the priests and soldiers were not his enemy that day; Satan was. Peter had a bigger fight in front of him. After the crucifixion and resurrection, Peter was to face the battle, rise up in Jesus' name, and build God's church. Now *that* was a battle worth fighting.

There is an unfair advantage for those who enter into a personal relationship with Jesus and, like Peter, will hear his voice as he guides us into knowing what fights we should and should not engage in. He is the only One who sees the big picture of our personal battle. When we try to do it without him, we go rogue and fight on our own. This can lead us to finding ourselves frustrated, fighting pointless fights with no victory. Like the old barrack fights in Twentynine Palms, we can fight but be completely oblivious to the real enemy and waste energy and focus. Yet, when we have an unfair advantage of trusting and hearing his voice, we will be able to be the warriors he created us to be and engage in the battle we were born to fight for our families, communities, our nation, and the kingdom of heaven.

A WARRIOR'S LEGACY

The only thing necessary for the triumph of evil
is for good men to do nothing.

ATTRIBUTED TO EDMUND BURKE

D ave and I stood alone in an empty enclosed concrete-and-tin garage within a small mud-wall compound in the tribal city of Jalalabad, Afghanistan. We were waiting to link up with the small team of elite special operators we were supporting that night, and it seemed to take forever for them to arrive. First, it was zero-dark thirty, and second, it was winter, and Afghanistan winters are brutal. The combination of cold weather and late hours always makes the hands of a clock feel like they are moving in slow motion.

When the team finally rolled up, Dave opened the garage door as I waved them in, and they all piled out of a small civilian Toyota van. I noticed that Afghan-style curtains blacked out the windows, a nice touch. As Dave shut the garage door behind them, I was surprised to see the team tactically peel out of the side door. Men the size of NFL linebackers, kitted up with the

most up-to-date gear, flawlessly secured the garage and interior rooms. Dave and I just watched and kind of chuckled. We had been living there for a week on our own, but these new arrivals were men I admired and looked up to, the best at their trade, so who was I to question their tactics?

I had previously worked with the senior enlisted operator in charge, and after he got the thumbs-up from his boys, all was good. His steely-eyed game face settled to a big smile as he walked over to shake Dave's and my hand and introduced me to some of the other boys. Through cursory greetings, the guys poked at us and said that we were insane to be alone in this area with the current increase in Taliban activity. As these guys called us "insane," Dave and I took their sarcasm as a compliment because these were some of the baddest warfighters on the planet. Like the line in *How the Grinch Stole Christmas*, "the Grinch's heart grew two sizes that day,"[16] I think Dave's and my ego did something similar.

As men, we want respect, especially among other peers whom we respect. This innate desire for respect is something that can drive men in one of two directions. It can inspire us to become great men or point us toward a life of destruction. The word *legacy* is a powerful word among men. We will *all* leave a legacy behind, but will it be something worthy? Your legacy can be one of a lost, angry, and bitter man, who, at his best, was *good* at his job, or it can be one of an honorable man, who served others, loved his family and friends, and never compromised his character or integrity. Will your legacy be one others who come behind you strive to emulate? The choice is yours. To achieve the desired results, we must choose the right path.

For most of us, it is far from easy to be a good man, let alone to leave a worthy legacy. As life goes by, it becomes increasingly

difficult to know what a good man *is*, yet it becomes increasingly more important to be that man. So how do we become "good men" if we do not even know what it means or have a marker in which to align ourselves as men? In retrospect of my own life, it is clear I spent a large portion of it believing the world revolved around *me*. I always had a heart for others, but selfishness put me at center stage for many years and kept me from really growing up. At Mighty Oaks, I see many men in the same situation.

Early in our programs, we ask our warriors a simple, yet challenging question: "When did you become a man?" The answers we receive are diverse, but all seem to revolve around a "macho" moment during their late teens or young adulthood: "When I got a job"…"When I joined the military"…"The first time I had sex"… "When I killed someone." The truth is that no single act in life transitions us into manhood, but there is a defining moment. The apostle Paul captured it best in 1 Corinthians 13:11, when he said, "When I was a child, I talked like a child, I thought like a child, I reasoned like a child. When I became a man, I put the ways of childhood behind me." There was a clear moment in Paul's life when he felt he walked out of childhood and into manhood. Through Mighty Oaks, as I observe so many men making the significant transition into manhood, the most consistent revelation in their lives has been that clear point when they walked away from their selfish ways and stepped into a life focused on serving others.

As men, God did not create us to be consumers but producers. It is woven in our souls to serve others and produce output into the world around us. However, I didn't come to this revelation the easy way. I took the long road and searched for many substitutes along the way to find the meaning of manhood. Some were good examples, but sadly, most were not so good. Most young boys should and do look to their fathers as a model of what a man

should be. In many cases, men replicate the shortfalls of their fathers as they continue generations of the same old mess, missing the mark. As was my case with my Marine Corps dad.

Coming home from Vietnam, he likely suffered the same anxieties and stresses that I faced when I returned from Afghanistan. A PTSD diagnosis, including government support, wasn't as available for returning service members at that time. Instead, many veterans of that era turned to alcohol, sex, and other paths of destruction. I'm one of thousands in the post-Vietnam generation to grow up with either an absent or dysfunctional father who was incapable of providing a model of manhood for their sons. At age seventeen, I was still longing for that positive example. Since I didn't see it modeled at home, I thought, *Where better to learn how to be a man than the United States Marine Corps, ooh rah?* Wow. How wrong could I have been?

Don't get me wrong, I *love* the Marines! Few things in my life have made me more proud than having earned the title of a United States marine. Yet, while the Marines do a phenomenal job of training young men for military service, they do not teach what it means to be an authentic man. Often, Marine Corps culture is rooted in a concept of masculinity that leaves the impression that the measure of manhood is based on how many beers you can guzzle, how many women you can sleep with, how many fights you can get in, and how many f-bombs you can squeeze into one sentence. Sadly, with the encouragement of this flawed masculinity comes the loss of many marines' careers over alcohol and domestic-violence incidents. I've witnessed good men who've lost rank over bar fights, lost their families through divorce over committing adultery, or picked up some sexually transmitted disease from some drunken one-night rendezvous. These behaviors are contrary to the core values of a marine: character, discipline, integrity, and honor.

My oldest son, Hunter, is a third-generation marine. When Hunter left for Marine Corps recruit training, I wrote him this letter to remind him of this, which he allowed me to share with you:

Son,

You are NOT going to the Marine Corps to learn how to be a man. You've already learned that from the model that God has laid out for you. Remember, they can teach you how to be a marine, and will, but you likely know far more than they do about being an authentic man, a Godly man of character. And, now, son, show them how to be THAT man and let God's light shine through you, to be an example to your fellow recruits and even your drill instructors. Remember, Joseph was a slave, but God gave him favor as a slave. God used him to bring hope and inspiration to Pharaoh, the king of Egypt! Even in the basement of a prison, locked away from the world, Paul was able, with God's guidance, to light a fire under humanity to build the kingdom of heaven. It's amazing how he can use the least of us. Just as in those moments in history, God is still working through those who believe in him. And he can and will use a nasty lil' Marine Corps recruit to bring hope and inspiration to each and every soul you encounter. Never discount where God may have you at that very moment for the very reason he put you here!

You are special and amazing!

I'm so proud of the man you've become and of your courage and boldness for him!

I love you,

Daddy

My dad passed away just a few months ago but not before Hunter became a marine. I called my dad while Hunter was in boot camp to tell him how Hunter was doing and that we would soon represent three generations of marines. He said, "They will make a man out of him," but I was happy to reply, "Too late, Dad. Hunter already is one." (By the way, not only did my dad and I find restoration, but I was honored to lead him to the Lord before his passing, and while we may not have had the best days together in this life, I am certain we will in eternity.)

Unlike Hunter, I found out what it meant to be a man in life only after almost losing it all. Yet, I changed the trajectory of my life and thus changed the legacy I will leave behind. By intentionally becoming the man God designed me to be, I have found fulfillment and a new sense of purpose. I've also discovered that being a man of God doesn't mean I must hang up my sword and turn in my "Man Card." To the contrary, God created men to be fighters. Just look at how many of our Bible heroes are warriors.

One of them was David. He frequented the battlefield, and the people praised him as a warrior, singing that David killed tens of thousands (1 Samuel 18:7). He also assembled a small group of elite special warriors known as David's Mighty Men, whom he led into battle after battle. David was eventually crowned king of Israel for his obedience to God's calling and his heroic actions as a warfighter and leader of men. But when we are first introduced to David in 1 Samuel 17, we see a boy becoming a man and then a warrior.

In that account, King Saul and the Israelites faced their mortal enemy, the Philistines. Each day, a nine-foot-tall Philistine giant and warfighting champion known as Goliath would come out to the battle line to mock the Israelite army, daring them to send forth a worthy

warrior to face off against him in one-on-one combat. King Saul and all his men were afraid; none was willing to take on the giant.

As chance (and God's providence) would have it, David (the young, freckled-faced boy, a poet and musician at heart, and a sheepherder by trade) happened to be at the battlefield that day, having taken a lunch to his older brothers in the army. When he heard the words of that giant, the warrior-spirit God had placed within him came to life. "David asked the men standing near him, 'What will be done for the man who kills this Philistine and removes this disgrace from Israel? Who is this uncircumcised Philistine that he should defy the armies of the living God?'" (v. 26).

David's brothers, hearing his questions, became angry and tried to make him go back and tend the sheep. But what he had seen and heard lit a fire inside David. At that moment, David faced what all men face in life: We see a problem and say, "Someone's got to do something about this! Who's going to act? Why not me?"

David volunteered to go fight the giant, but King Saul belittled him—he was just a boy and Goliath was a seasoned warrior; he wouldn't stand a chance!

> "But David said to Saul, 'Your servant has been keeping his father's sheep. When a lion or a bear came and carried off a sheep from the flock, I went after it, struck it and rescued the sheep from its mouth. When it turned on me, I seized it by its hair, struck it and killed it. Your servant has killed both the lion and the bear; this uncircumcised Philistine will be like one of them, because he has defied the armies of the living God. The Lord who rescued me from the paw of the lion and the paw of the bear will rescue me from the hand of this Philistine." (vv. 34–37)

Whoa! We have ourselves a fighter. I'm sure King Saul (and everyone else who saw this going down) called David insane. Only, David wasn't insane. He had an unfair advantage. David didn't care how big Goliath was because he understood how big God was, and that made the difference. That knowledge gave him the courage he needed to face the giant that no one else would.

King Saul finally agreed to let young David try. After all, nobody else was doing anything. But then Saul wanted David to do it Saul's way and with Saul's armor rather than the unorthodox way David had always used and been successful with. It is almost comical trying to visualize the scene of King Saul and his men attempting to dress the small boy in the king's large tunic, armor, and helmet. It was obviously too big. David said, "I cannot go in these," and took them off. He kept only his staff and his sling, choosing five smooth stones from the streambed (some say he chose five stones because the giant had brothers).

When the giant saw this puny kid coming toward him, he was offended and began to mock David, attempting to intimidate him:

> "Am I a dog, that you come at me with sticks?" And the Philistine cursed David by his gods. "Come here," he said, "and I'll give your flesh to the birds and the wild animals!" David said to the Philistine, "You come against me with sword and spear and javelin, but I come against you in the name of the LORD Almighty, the God of the armies of Israel, whom you have defied. This day the LORD will deliver you into my hands, and I'll strike you down and cut off your head. This very day I will give the carcasses of the Philistine army to the birds and the wild animals, and the whole world will know that there is a God in Israel. All those gath-

ered here will know that it is not by sword or spear that the Lord saves; for the battle is the Lord's, and he will give all of you into our hands." (vv. 43–47)

David had an unfair advantage that comes from knowing that God is on your side in battle. As the giant approached, "David ran quickly toward the battle line to meet him" (v. 48). David drew a stone, loaded his slingshot, and threw it, striking Goliath so hard on the forehead that the stone sunk down into his skull. The giant fell facedown onto the ground. David stood over him, took the giant's massive sword from its sheath, and chopped off Goliath's head for all to see. The Philistine army was struck by fear and began a quick retreat.

The great evangelist Billy Graham once said, "Courage is contagious. When a brave man takes a stand, the spines of others are often stiffened."[17] Indeed. When David slew the giant, the frightened Israelites decided that they, too, would rise up and fight. They pursued the fleeing Philistine army, killing them all along the way. The Bible says dead Philistines were strung up for display along Shaaraim road as far as the cities of Gath and Ekron. With God's help, David left behind a worthy legacy.

We all will leave behind a legacy, and it will be a good legacy—if you live out God's intent for you. But being the man and the warrior you were created to be is a great challenge, and you will face giants of your own. If you're not fighting, then you will be a victim. Had David not answered God's call in his life, we wouldn't even know his name now. What would his legacy have been?

I want my legacy to be one worthy to be remembered, and I want others to follow my example. I want my legacy to be one of a man who embraced a warrior's life on and off the battlefield. I want to be remembered as a man who served others and who fought

daily to be the husband, father, friend, and man God intended me to be and that in all I have done in this life, the most significant will have been pointing others to him and leading others to do the same.

What about you? What will your legacy be?

CHAPTER 15

THE GOOD FIGHT

Pray also for me, that whenever I speak, words may be given
me so that I will fearlessly make known the mystery of the
gospel, for which I am an ambassador in chains.
Pray that I may declare it fearlessly, as I should.

EPHESIANS 6:19–20

Deep in the mountainous region of the Federally Administered Tribal Areas (FATA) that merged Afghanistan and
Pakistan, Andy, Shahr, and I drove along a canyon wall in
an open-topped Jeep. Everything seemed sketchy. The road was
barely attached to the canyon side and not really wide enough for
the Jeep's wheelbase. We were dangling hundreds of feet over
the canyon floor, the Jeep was old, and I'm pretty sure it hadn't
had a brake job in twenty years—if ever.

The driver, a local to the area who was maybe fifteen years
old, seemed to want to be a tour guide, pointing at sights in the
countryside. Shahr had lived in these mountains most of his life
and seemed to be content, but I had no shame in expressing my

uneasiness about plunging off the ledge and asked Shahr to tell the driver to shut up and keep his eyes on the road.

When we finally made our way past the cliff, we entered a picturesque, wide-open, lush and green high-mountain valley. It was a breathtakingly beautiful place, making it hard to imagine that danger lurked there, but it did not fool me. I knew better—I knew that evil was undoubtedly present.

As we paused to take in the beauty of the valley and let our blood pressure settle from the death-defying drive, Andy took a moment for a photo-op. In addition to having spent more than twenty years in special operations, he was an avid outdoorsman and loved nature and photography. He must have gotten caught in the moment, however, and made a major cultural error when he snapped a few pictures of children playing in the river. This was a definite no-no in this region.

Out of nowhere, I heard a woman screaming. It was clearly an angry rant. I looked toward the voice and noticed an old lady, followed by two younger tribal men, running straight toward us. The men were laughing and didn't seem intimidating, but the old lady was not laughing at all. She was enraged and had fire in her eyes. As she ran across the riverbed, she picked up two soft-ball-sized river rocks, one for each hand, and continued to charge our way. Shahr said, "She's yelling about the pictures you took!" He looked scared, but he gave us good advice not to fight back or touch her but to be careful because she was serious and so was the situation. She had covered a lot of ground quickly for an older lady, and as she approached us, the two accompanying men were trying to calm her while laughing about the situation. I'm glad they thought it was funny because it was clear things were escalating quickly.

Enraged, she came straight at us, still with fire in her eyes.

She had her arms raised with those river rocks in hand, and she launched one right at us. She had a pretty good arm, and we weren't going to stand still for more incoming rocks. Here we were, three rough-and-tough alpha-predator dudes—one lifelong mountain man and two seasoned special operators—face-to-face with an old village lady, and we began cowardly running away from her in a circle around the Jeep. We continued for several laps, running in circles as she chased us. There were a few moments when we cut each other off and got behind one another. I could imagine how funny a sight this was to the two men observing and laughing. This had to look like a Keystone Cops circus act. The men and Shahr continued to try to calm her. She finally stopped chasing but faked a throw several times just to play with us.

The two men were able to get her to drop the final rock and escorted her away from us, still laughing as they walked off. In the War on Terror, Andy and I lost a battle of courage that day to a seventy-plus-year-old tribal lady who had our number (and a pretty good arm as well!).

There are times to be courageous and bold, and there are times to be humble and refrain from fighting until another day. There will also be times when we fight and fail or even when we fail to try at all. But regardless, at any moment we can step out of our past and directly into the future that God has for us.

Luke, a physician by trade, became a close companion to the apostle Paul and wrote the book of Acts. He documented the courageous and bold actions of the early pioneers who shared the gospel of Jesus and started the Christian church and who did so during a period when neither was popular. At that time, you could be put to death for spreading the message of Jesus' ministry.

One of the main players in Acts was Peter, who with great boldness helped to launch the church. But his earlier actions

had not reflected or predicted the strong man that he would later become. Peter was initially known as a man of big talk but with actions that fell far short. For example, Jesus wanted to see who was bold enough to declare his existence at a time when there was stiff opposition to Jesus and the movement he was leading. Peter boldly stood up and answered, "You are the Messiah, the Son of the living God!" (Matthew 16:16). This was a forceful declaration that could have been a death sentence in many circles of that day, yet Peter made that pronouncement without hesitation. It was at that moment Jesus declared Peter would be the "rock" and a key figure he would use to build his church. Yet, Peter's boldness would crumble into gross cowardice in the days to come, and he would fail.

Prior to Jesus' arrest and crucifixion, he forewarned Peter, face-to-face, "You will all fall away." Peter quickly responded, "Even if all fall away, I will not!" But, Jesus replied, "Truly I tell you, … before the rooster crows twice you yourself will disown me three times." "No!" Peter declared emphatically. "Even if I have to die with you, I will never disown you!" (Mark 14:27, 29–31).

Only hours later, Jesus was arrested, and Peter quickly denied Jesus three times, just as Jesus had predicted—even once to a little girl. Peter had talked a big game but had crumbled on game day. Many of us have been there.

Do you think Jesus didn't know that? Jesus knew Peter would fail to stand by him. Author John Maxwell accurately observed, "God uses people who fail, cause there aren't any other kind around."[18] Jesus knew who Peter was—the good, the bad, and the ugly—yet he chose him anyway. He entrusted Peter with one of the most crucial missions any man on earth could ever be given.

After Peter witnessed the crucifixion of Jesus, he was dev-

astated, but he had a visit from the risen Jesus. Jesus let Peter know that he was still entrusted with the important mission he had called him to and that even though he had rejected Jesus and messed up, Jesus still wanted Peter on the team.

God wants to use each of us for his purpose, regardless of our past (or even future). He has an important mission for us—a warrior's mission. He has a great spiritual battle that you were created and commissioned to be a part of: "For our struggle is not against flesh and blood, but against the rulers, against the authorities, against the powers of this dark world and against the spiritual forces of evil in the heavenly realms" (Ephesians 6:12). Peter accepted this and became the man Jesus knew he could be.

In Acts 3, Peter, along with the apostle John, was going up to the temple at prayer time. They came across a forty-year-old crippled man who, for his entire life, had begged at the temple. When the beggar saw Peter and John about to enter, he asked them for money. Peter looked straight at him and said, "'Look at us!' So the man gave them his attention, expecting to get something from them. Then Peter said, 'Silver or gold I do not have, but what I do have I give you. In the name of Jesus Christ of Nazareth, walk.' Taking him by the right hand, he helped him up, and instantly the man's feet and ankles became strong. He jumped to his feet and began to walk" (vv. 4–8).

Peter did this at the same temple wherein resided the religious leaders who had recently crucified Jesus. And now, in the name of Jesus, Peter healed a known cripple in their front yard. Everyone, including the healed man, started talking. Peter had openly professed the resurrection of the Messiah. To the religious leaders, this was a blatant act of blasphemy, and therefore, Peter could be imprisoned, tortured, and brutally crucified, just like

Jesus. I'm not sure that Peter was intentionally picking a fight, but nonetheless, a fight was on.

In Acts 4, the religious leaders sent the temple guards to arrest Peter and John and bring them to a public trial within the temple. During such trials, the religious leaders would stand together, dressed in their fancy attire, and encircle the accused to intimidate them. Then they would hurl questions and accusations at them to confuse them and to pressure and coerce them into some sort of confession for their crimes, at which time they would immediately sentence them to their punishment.

Menacingly, the leaders encircled Peter and John, confronting them, demanding: "By what power or what name did you do this?" (v. 7). The new Peter was not in the least fearful or intimidated. He welcomed their challenge and threw their question right back at them: "Then Peter, filled with the Holy Spirit, said to them, 'Rulers and elders of the people! If we are being called to account today for an act of kindness shown to a man who was lame and are being asked how he was healed, then know this, you and all the people of Israel: It is by the name of Jesus Christ of Nazareth, whom you crucified but whom God raised from the dead, that this man stands before you healed'" (vv. 8–10). *Wow!* This was not the same man who had previously flip-flopped in hard times. Jesus believed in this Peter all along, the rock.

Peter not only confessed to healing the man but also declared Jesus as the Christ and even condemned the religious leaders as murderers, affirming that Jesus had indeed risen from the dead. This was all the religious leaders needed to condemn Peter and John—except they were so shocked they didn't know how to respond: "When they saw the courage of Peter and John and realized that they were unschooled, ordinary men, they were astonished and they took note that these men had been with

Jesus" (v. 13). When an enemy stands face-to-face with some-one who holds that kind of courage—a courage found in the deep belief that one is called by God himself—they often don't know how to respond.

The crowd at the temple was fired up. They were cheering for Peter and John.

When people get "punked out" in public, they often try to backpedal and save face, which is what the religious leaders did. They told Peter and John that they were going to give them a pass on this one—as long as they never spoke about Jesus again. "But Peter and John replied, 'Which is right in God's eyes: to listen to you, or to him? You be the judges! As for us, we cannot help speaking about what we have seen and heard'" (vv. 19–20). The leaders then blustered and threatened them further but had to release them because they didn't know how to punish them without starting a riot.

Peter was no longer all talk. He had become the bold warrior God created him to be. That day five thousand people became followers of Jesus. Jesus knew Peter would become the man and warrior he was created to be, even though all the evidence prior to that time pointed in the other direction.

Becoming the warrior and leader God created you to be begins with starting your own personal relationship with Jesus Christ and aligning your life to his will. Without that, you'll always have a hole deep in your soul. But when you truly align your life to his will, you will discover an unfair advantage in every battle you face from that moment forward. Regardless of any difficulties to come, you will be a warrior who cannot be defeated, no matter the outcome.

However, you must know that when you stand in your right-ful role as a warrior of God, you will certainly face opposition,

just as Peter did. This is how we know we are in the right place. As Jesus explained, "If the world hates you, keep in mind that it hated me first. If you belonged to the world, it would love you as its own. As it is, you do not belong to the world, but I have chosen you out of the world. That is why the world hates you. Remember what I told you: 'A servant is not greater than his master.' If they persecuted me, they will persecute you also. If they obeyed my teaching, they will obey yours also" (John 15:18–20).

When you choose to "fight the good fight" (as the apostle Paul called it in 1 Timothy 6:12), the enemy will come at you like an old, crazy tribal lady armed with river rocks in her hands and fire in her eyes. Be ready to fight the good fight with everything you have. Your enemy is fierce, but the reward is great.

I share these lessons with you warrior to warrior—just as if I were handing off an AO (area of operation) that I had been working in Afghanistan with a left seat/right seat turnover so that you will have an unfair advantage by being prepared for the attacks that come with a life of faith. Others prepared me in this way, and when the attacks come, it makes the victory that much sweeter.

COURAGE BEYOND FEAR

Have I not commanded you?
Be strong and courageous.
Do not be afraid; do not be discouraged,
for the LORD your God will be with you wherever you go.

JOSHUA 1:9

I have done much and been through much, and many times, I was not only scared but also terrified. But I steadied my trembling knees and pressed on, just as many other warriors before me have done and will do after me.

John Wayne is famous for having said, "Courage is being scared to death and saddling up anyway." I have worked among some of the military's most courageous warriors, and I have worked with real-life heroes who committed their lives to service as patriots in defense of America or in defense of our neighbors in a foreign land who couldn't defend themselves from the evil of this world. I have also heard hundreds of firsthand accounts of courage, sacrifice, and valor, often coming at great risk of injury

or death, and in some cases with death as the actual cost. As I examine my own story, I often measure my attempts to be brave against others who have blazed a way before me, trying to live up to the standard they set.

With my military assignments, there was a moment when I came to a clear realization that I would probably be killed or captured. As part of my task force, I often found myself working alone with local nationals, with little or no support if something went wrong. I had extensive training, a keen knowledge of the area and culture, and the confidence to do my job, but over time, the fears and realities of what I was doing rose to the surface.

A Bible verse that many often associate with the military is John 15:13: "Greater love has no one than this: to lay down one's life for one's friends." Guys get the tattoo; it's on T-shirts and painted on walls and on banners. It's a motivating verse, but most of us don't go beyond the "Rah! Rah!" associated with that verse and actually ponder what our final moment of life will be or what comes next. Envisioning your own funeral or the thought of your family going on without you or your wife remarrying and your children having a new dad and you becoming just a memory to them can all be overwhelming and make you question your will to continue.

Many nights I went to sleep and my mind would wander into visions of being mortally wounded and bleeding out in some muddy Afghan ditch with my body being mutilated by a people who hold a deep hatred for us. And even worse than dying were the thoughts of living—of being captured and my feet smashed in with sledgehammers, skin carved off my body, being raped and tortured for months, possibly years.

I have been trained—and have even trained others, as both a warrior and a professional fighter—never to visualize defeat, only

victory. But the very real possibility that I might be only moments away from these fears becoming reality weighed heavily against the bravado that I was somehow immune to these dangers. As warriors, we push these tormenting thoughts way down inside us somewhere and saddle up anyway, but for me, it became more than I could bear at times.

I've been asked on numerous occasions, "When did your PTSD start? What happened? Was there an incident that set it off?" When I came home from my final deployment, I spoke to a psychologist once a week for nearly a year, and we could never put a finger on one incident—and to this day I still can't. I could attribute the answer to those questions to many incidents, but I can say with complete confidence that for me it started the moment I allowed fear to settle in. When fear took root, it was like a cancer, and it eroded my strength, my confidence, my will, and my ability to do my job. I worked to fight it off, but the reality of the old recon marine saying that "The anticipation of drowning is worse than drowning itself" became true for me. The fear of what I faced became a real and overwhelming reality of imminent doom.

As I look back, there were several indications that should have warned me about the state of fear that was overtaking me. I would often leave wherever I was operating out of and head out for multi-day or week trips to complete a mission-related task, typically with a small group of men and into remote tribal areas overrun with bad guys. When leaving on these trips, I would write short notes for my family: *Kathy, I love you. You're such a great mom and you will be fine.* Or, *Hunter, Daddy loves you. You will have to take care of the family now. I trust you and know you can do it.* The notes were different each time but always had the same tone of message for Kathy, Hunter, Haili, and Hayden. I would place the notes in my suitcase so that they would be immediately

visible when opened, hoping that my personal effects would make it home to them when I didn't.

Each time I made it back safely I would throw the notes away. I didn't want Kathy to ever find them and share in the experience of my fear. There were numerous moments when I knew I would die, and in retrospect, it is miraculous that I didn't. Most warriors who have been in places like Iraq, Afghanistan, Vietnam, and other war zones share the same experience that regardless of our personal fear, we press forward in the belief that the price of the sacrifice is worth the cost. And even for those who don't accept that reasoning, at least being there for the guy next to you is worth the price. This is what a warrior does.

While I share with others the stories of amazing warriors in the Bible, I think the enemy makes a deliberate attempt to hide the truth that the toughest and most courageous warrior in the Scriptures is Jesus himself. Many portray a caricature of Jesus as a wimpy, peace-love-and-happiness guy, skipping around Jerusalem with a white robe and beautiful flowing hair, healing the sick and simply loving everyone unconditionally. But that is not a true picture of Jesus.

I have found no greater standard of courage than Jesus Christ at Calvary when he faced crucifixion. For days, months, and even years before, his anticipation was building to that moment. The clock was ticking for him to face his brutal destiny and death. Jesus, the Son of God and the Messiah, had a clear mission directive to trade his life for ours. He was to be the sacrificial Lamb for all the sins of the world. He was intimately aware of the Old Testament teaching and prophecies concerning the sacrificial death that he would face. Jesus was fully a man, and he experienced the same life, hardship, and anguish that the rest of

us do. He didn't exempt himself from the physical pain, emotions, and physiological effects of the human body.

The one advantage Jesus did have during his human life was the same *unfair advantage* spoken of throughout this book: the advantage that comes when you upgrade your faith for belief. It comes when you move from a vague hope to absolute certainty and conviction—from saying to yourself, *I hope things will turn out right* to having the unwavering confidence that through God everything is going to be completely right, regardless of how things seem to turn out.

We don't know exactly when Jesus discovered who he was, but we know from the Bible that he did and thus had an unfair advantage of living without fear once he knew who he was. Fear comes from being uncertain of the unknown; Jesus did not face the unknown. He was keenly aware of what was before him. I wonder if that knowledge ever kept him up at night. Did he struggle with the anguish of what he would face?

Remember the recon saying "The anticipation of drowning is worse than drowning itself"? Jesus lived his entire life knowing he would not only endure false accusations, arrest, torture, and a brutal murder, but he would also face rejection from his own creation—those who he loved the most. Despite this, he went forward with his mission.

In Matthew 26, we see a glimpse of Jesus dealing with the difficulties he was about to face. After the Last Supper (his last meal before his execution), he went off with some of his disciples to the Garden of Gethsemane and told them: "My soul is overwhelmed with sorrow to the point of death. Stay here and keep watch with me" (v. 38). Jesus walked off to pray and fell to his face on the ground, praying, "My Father, if it is possible, may this cup be taken from me. Yet not as I will, but as you will" (v. 39).

Jesus continued praying for over an hour, pacing back and forth, and three times he told God: "My Father, if it is not possible for this cup to be taken away unless I drink it, may your will be done" (v. 42). Luke's writings visualize Jesus' extreme anguish of this moment: "His sweat was like drops of blood falling to the ground" (Luke 22:44).

Jesus "returned to the disciples and said to them, 'Are you still sleeping and resting? Look, the hour has come, and the Son of Man is delivered into the hands of sinners. Rise! Let us go! Here comes my betrayer!'" (Matthew 26:45–46).

Courage is not the absence of fear but rather the decision that something is more important than that fear and moving on anyway. There is no example in history of courage greater than this: Jesus voluntarily delivered himself into the hands of his enemies to pay the ultimate price for humanity—for each of us. Jesus didn't turn himself over to his enemies because he was weak; he turned himself over to them because he was strong. Even the bravest of us would run or maybe fight back in one last attempt to beat destiny, but Jesus bravely embraced his. In his final moments during the intense pain and horror of crucifixion, Jesus spoke several words. The final and most powerful was his affirmation that his mission was complete when he said in Greek, "*Tetelestai,*" or "It is finished" (John 19:30). But before these final words, he said something that can be confusing if not understood: "*Eli, Eli, lama sabachthani*?," or "My God, my God, why have you forsaken me?" (Matthew 27:46).

I've heard it asked, "Why would Jesus say this? Did he really believe God had forsaken him?" No; he said it because "*Eli, Eli, lama sabachthani*" is the Aramaic title of Psalm 22, which is a prophecy of the crucifixion—but it was written a thousand years before Christ was born by someone who had never witnessed

a crucifixion because crucifixion hadn't even been invented yet! Nevertheless, the author of Psalm 22 narrated the crucifixion with accuracy a millennium before it occurred. It was indeed divine and showed why Jesus would reference it:

> My God, my God, why have you forsaken me? Why are you so far from saving me, so far from my cries of anguish?…But I am a worm and not a man, scorned by everyone, despised by the people. All who see me mock me; they hurl insults, shaking their heads. "He trusts in the LORD," they say, "let the LORD rescue him. Let him deliver him, since he delights in him."… Many bulls surround me; strong bulls of Bashan encircle me. Roaring lions that tear their prey open their mouths wide against me. I am poured out like water, and all my bones are out of joint. My heart has turned to wax; it has melted within me. My mouth is dried up like a potsherd, and my tongue sticks to the roof of my mouth; you lay me in the dust of death. Dogs surround me, a pack of villains encircles me; they pierce my hands and my feet. All my bones are on display; people stare and gloat over me. They divide my clothes among them and cast lots for my garment.…They will proclaim his righteousness, declaring to a people yet unborn: He has done it! (excerpts from Psalm 22:1–31)

It was finished. The prophesy was fulfilled, and Jesus' mission was complete.

Jesus had the unfair advantage of knowing who he was and what he was here to do. For any of us, the foreknowledge of such a mission would have been too heavy a burden to carry. Yet Jesus

chose to do it anyway. He took on the ultimate battle for humanity, and his heroic actions have eternally saved us all, if we will rely on him and conform our will to his. Why did he do it? Because he wanted to. He did it for us—for you. He is the perfect warrior who demonstrates courage under fire in a way we can all strive to emulate as we face our own times of fear, anxiety, and doubt.

I pray you have already made the decision to be in a relationship with Christ and align your life to his plan for you so that you can face your battles wearing the full armor of God. If you haven't made that choice yet, I pray this book has challenged, encouraged, and inspired you to do so. (If you want more information about how to be in a personal relationship with Jesus, check out Resource #1 at the end.) When I made that choice, I found my purpose—the very reason God created me—and I discovered an unfair advantage that led me to victory in the midst of my battles. I pray *you* discover that same advantage for the battles you face and unlock the warrior spirit sewn into *your* heart by God himself.

1980
I was always
a fighter and
started martial
arts at five
years old.

1995
Traditional
Marine Corps
Wedding in Sun
City, California.

1995
The typical cold and
wet day at Basic
Reconnaissance
Course in California
(see Chapter 5).

1999
My gold wing
jump at 3rd
Force Recon
Company.
"Hurry up
and wait."

1999
USMC Birthday
Ball at 3rd
Force Recon
Company.

2004
The eerie site
of "The Killing
Pool" (see
Chapter 1).

2004
A teammate and me in eastern Afghanistan.

2004
Local Kabul transportation.

2005
A teammate and me in the FATA Region with a Toyota Prado.

2005
Shopping on Chicken Street with "Bob" (see Chapter 4).

2005
Golf day in Kabul, Afghanistan
(see Chapter 4).

2005
A rainy Afghanistan
day before the crazy
events in Chapter 7.

2006
Father's Day while I was
away in Afghanistan.

2007
My Land Rover in
the Valley of the
Shadow of Death
(see Chapter 4).

2007

Such a beautiful yet evil place
(see Chapter 4).

2007
Winter Mountains
kicking my butt
(see Chapter 4).

2009
Inaugural Legacy FC World Title Championship (from left, Lewis "The General" Woods, Prof. "Draculino," Todd Moore, me, and Daniel Kim).

2010
Me *vs* Humberto Deleon, StrikeForce at Houston Toyota Center (see Chapter 9). Photo courtesy of Dave Manuel.

2010
Brawling with Humberto in StrikeForce. Photo courtesy of Dave Manuel.

2010
Getting knocked on my butt by Humberto at StrikeForce. Photo courtesy of Dave Manuel.

2010
I kicked Humberto in the face three times, but he wouldn't go down. Photo courtesy of Dave Manuel.

2011

Hard fought battle against Bellator FC Champion Zach Makovsky. Photo courtesy of Dave Manuel.

2012

Touching gloves with Sandoval at Legacy FC (see Chapter 12). Photo courtesy of Mike Calimbas.

2012

Celebrating victory over UFC Fighter Joseph Sandoval at Legacy FC. Photo courtesy of Mike Calimbas.

2012

"Fight for the microphone." Legacy FC on HD Net and interviewing with UFC Hall of Famer Pat Miletich (see Chapter 12). Photo courtesy of Andy Hemingway

2013

Battling with Andrew Yates at NBC Sports World Series of Fighting. Photo courtesy of Lucas Noonan, WSOF.

2013

Giving glory to God at NBC Sports World Series of Fighting. Photo courtesy of Lucas Noonan, WSOF.

2013

Praying over my fallen brothers Foster and Robert's name on the War on Terror Memorial Wall prior to speaking.

2015

The "Robo" Family.

2015

Hunter became the third generation Robichaux Marine.

2015

Haili, my precious daughter and friend.

2015

From left, MOWP's Jeremy Stalnecker (Afterword), Lt. Gen. "Jerry" Boykin (Foreword), me, and David Barton (Contributor) at a MOWP Gala in Texas.

2016

Chad and Kathy with Airmen from the USAF 482nd Fighter Wing during a Resiliency Event.

2016

I love when "The Robo Boys" get to train together. My two sons are my pride and my joy. From left, Hayden, me, and Hunter.

2016

Saying goodbye to my dad and former marine, Danny, shortly before he passed.

2016

Taking down Geoff Real at Fight to Win Pro. Photo courtesy of Mike Calimbas.

2017

Kathy and me spreading the word of MOWP in California.

2017
Steve Toth (mentor) came to hear me speak in Texas (see Chapter 11).

2017
With MOWP Graduates at Blaylock Ranch in Texas.

2017
Earning my 3rd Degree Black Belt from the legendary Carlson Gracie Jr. with friends, fellow black belts, Tom, Sean, and Tino at Carlson Gracie Temecula.

2017
Sharing a message of spiritual resiliency to the Warriors of 5th Marines prior to their deployment to Afghanistan.

BIBLIOGRAPHY

1   "MMA Rankings, Records and Statistics," Fight Matrix, https://www.fightmatrix.com/fighter-profile/Chad+Robichaux/5388/.

2   National Association of Boxing Commissions Official MMA Fighter Database, https://wwwmixedmartialarts.com/fighter/Chad-Robichaux:6460965746C3CC75. "Chad Robichaux 'Robo'," Sherdog.com, https://www.sherdog.com/fighter/Chad-Robichaux-25199.

3   "Medals of Valor: Detectives Cantelli & Robichaux," St. Charles Sheriff's Department Archives, https://www.stcharlessheriff.org/DocumentCenter/Home/View/47.

4   Tim McGirk, "Beware of Land Mines On the First Fairway," *Time* Magazine, November 21, 2005.

5   https://www.blueletterbible.org

6   US Marine Corps Association and Foundation, https://www.mca-marines.org/leatherneck/bookreview/devil-dogs-belleau-wood-us-marines-world-war-i.

7   "Medals of Valor: Detectives Cantelli & Robichaux," St. Charles Sheriff's Department Archives, https://www.stcharlessheriff.org.

8   Robert E. Howard, *Tower of the Elephant: The Coming of Conan the Cimmerian*, (CreateSpace Independent Publishing, 2014), back cover.

9   John Eldredge, *Beautiful Outlaw*, (FaithWords, 2011), 40, e-book.

10 "MMA Rankings, Records and Statistics," Fight Matrix, https://www.fightmatrix.com/fighter-profile/Chad+Robichaux/5388/.

11 "Saddam: 'New Mongols' face defeat," CNN.com, https://www.cnn.com/2003/WORLD/meast/01/17/sproject.irq.saddam/.

12 "VA Conducts Nation's Largest Analysis of Veteran Suicide," US Department of Veteran Affairs, https://www.va.gov/opa/pressrel/pressrelease.cfm?id=2801.

13   Thomas James Brennan, "Inside the Painstaking Recovery Process of a Medal of Honor Marine," *Vanity Fair*, https://www.vanityfair.com/news/2016/11/medal-of-honor-marine-recovery.

14   Stu Weber, *Tender Warrior: Every Man's Purpose, Every Woman's Dream, Every Child's Hope,* (Multnomah Books, 1993), 247–248.

15   Ed Rapphun, "No Decision May Be Worst Decision," *The Tennessean*, https://www.tennessean.com/story/money/2014/07/28/decision-may-worst-decision/13243769/.

16   *Dr. Seuss' How the Grinch Stole Christmas,* Universal Studios, 2000.

17   Harold Myra and Marshall Shelley, *The Leadership Secrets of Billy Graham*, (Zondervan, 2005), 164.

18   John C. Maxwell and Thomas Nelson, *The Complete 101 Collection: What Every Leader Needs to Know*, (Reprint edition, 2015), 60.

BY JEREMY M. STALNECKER

BUILDING A WALL

I am carrying on a great project and cannot go down.
Why should the work stop while I leave it and go down to you?

NEHEMIAH 6:3

I often hear people talk about how difficult it was for them to figure out what they wanted to do with their lives. One day they want to be a policeman, a doctor the next, and then maybe a movie star the day after. I have a hard time understanding this because the only thing that I ever wanted to be was a United States marine. My childhood dream finally came true when I was commissioned as a Second Lieutenant in the Marine Corps.

After a year of training, I finally stepped in front of my first infantry platoon as a member of Charlie Company, First Battalion, Fifth Marines at Camp Pendleton. I spent the next two years

training with this platoon until I was moved to Weapons Company and became the counter-mechanized platoon commander.

For those who have been around the Marine Corps, counter-mech included heavy machine guns, TOW (tube-launched, optically-tracked, wire-guided antitank missile systems), and Javelin anti-tank missile systems. We had enough marines and equipment to act as our own company, and we trained hard and became extremely proficient at our craft. The time came to put all that training to good use.

My platoon, along with about thirty thousand other marines from the First Marine Division, deployed to Kuwait in preparation for a probable invasion into Iraq in response to the 9/11 terrorist attacks on New York City and Washington, DC. The mission launched on March 20, 2003, as thousands of US Military warriors moved across the border and began to secure strategic objectives.

Our battalion was tasked with breeching the berm between Iraq and Kuwait on what would become the center axis of advance toward Baghdad. The first three days of the war were some of the craziest of my life. Having tracer rounds coming our direction was new to us. We obviously knew this would happen, but it still felt completely out of place when it did. I learned many lessons during my time there, and one of the biggest ones was that good training does indeed take over when everything else seems out of control.

As our time in Iraq unfolded, the pendulum swung between long periods of boredom and moments with so much adrenaline that I could stay awake for days. But through it all, I never lost sight of the fact that I needed to do everything within my power to bring home all the marines in my platoon.

After securing our first objective, our next destination was the capital city of Baghdad. There were many major engagements and other objectives along the way, but we all knew the

battle would end in one of the largest cities in the Middle East. Our battalion fought our way into that enormous city and took over the presidential palace on the north side of the Tigris River.

One of my most prized possessions is a picture of our platoon standing in front of the rubble of one of the buildings on the palace grounds. That picture represents the fact that we had an unbelievable job to do and did it—without losing a man.

For a marine in combat, the mission is always first, and a close second is making sure that the people in your care will get to see their families again. For years after returning home, I would reflect on my days in service and feel a sense of pride for having achieved both of those objectives.

When I left the Marines, I went into full-time Christian ministry. My first year after returning from Iraq was very hard. There had been no time for reintegration from military back into civilian life, so to make the transition, I felt like I had to move as far away as possible from my time in uniform, both mentally and emotionally. Practically, that meant that I made no effort to keep in touch with any of the marines I had served alongside. I really believed that when I put my uniform in the closet for the last time, I had done my job and my obligation to First Battalion Fifth Marines had ended. I had little desire to look back. But that all changed when I saw several of those men again almost ten years later.

I had become the pastor of a church in the city of Fremont near San Francisco. My family and I had been there for a few years and had adjusted well to life in that type of ministry. Unless I told people that I had served, they wouldn't have known. I was proud of my service, but I was just as happy not to make it a big part of my life. One of the interesting things about the Bay Area of California is that there are not a lot of veterans. We had a few in our church, but they were definitely the exception.

One afternoon, I received a message from one of the marines in my platoon who had somehow tracked me down. He asked me to call him because he thought that I'd be interested in a special opportunity. He told me of someone he knew from Houston, Texas, who had recently started a program for veterans with PTSD. He didn't know much about the program but was told that if he could get some guys from the old platoon together, they would do a session just for us.

I checked on the founder, Chad Robichaux, and saw that he had a pretty diverse background. At that time, there was not a lot of information about him available outside of his professional fighting career. I did learn that he was trying to leverage his military background to minister to struggling veterans. I didn't consider myself a struggling veteran, but I decided that it would be good to see some of the platoon again and that maybe I could learn something that could be useful at my church. And so, I traveled to Westcliffe, Colorado, for my first Mighty Oaks Warrior Programs session.

That week, I spent time with marines I had not seen in nearly ten years, and I did learn some things I was able to use at my church. But I also discovered that there were some things in my own life that still lingered from my time in combat that I needed to deal with. I realized that we are all broken to some extent, and it was good to remember that so we could continue to grow.

But the most unexpected revelation for me that week was that many marines from the old platoon had struggled since coming home. I heard stories of those who had made a way for themselves and were doing well, but I also heard about suicides, broken homes, and shipwrecked lives. My biggest takeaway was that my responsibility to them should not have ended when my official service time did.

As I listened to them talk, I realized that if we—those who have served—don't take care of one another, then no one else will. We get upset with the VA (Veterans Affairs) and other government organizations, but the reality is that we need to be responsible for standing up and providing solutions for the brokenness that our brothers are dealing with. We first need to find help personally and then work to pay it forward for others.

Paying It Forward

Mighty Oaks was born out of the simple concept that we need to be responsible for others who have served. The idea of paying it forward is what I have always appreciated about Mighty Oaks and its methodology—this is part of its DNA. When Chad began teaching others what God had used in his life to restore so many broken pieces, he was modeling this non-negotiable principle that has been passed on to tens of thousands of people. (You can read the whole "The Mighty Oaks Journey" in the resource section of this book).

People ask often, "How do you, in only a few days, do what so many other programs cannot do in weeks or months?" The answer is that it is not what happens in a few days; it is what happens the moment a man or woman decides to get up and become the person who he or she was created to be. This seems way too simple, but that is the power in paying it forward.

I have been involved with the programs of Mighty Oaks since the first one I attended, and I eventually left the church I was pastoring to become part of the team and am now the executive director. I've seen the program grow, and people come and go, but God has blessed it through every transition. The goal has remained to use personal experiences, good and bad, as a plat-

form to help veterans (and active-duty service members and their families) to find their true God-given purpose. When that happens, each of us can begin to invest in the people who God has placed in our lives—a process that, if done correctly, will never end.

I Cannot Go Down

The work we do at Mighty Oaks Warrior Programs is illustrated in the book of Nehemiah. Throughout the history of the nation of Israel, there were good times and dark times. When Israel followed God, his hand of blessing was on them, and they prospered. When they turned their backs on him, his judgment replaced his blessing. During periods of judgment, it was common for Israel to fall under the tyranny of other nations. They would lose their sovereignty and become the servants or, more appropriately, the slaves of pagan countries and their leaders.

During these dark periods, foreign kings would set up their leadership in the homeland of the Israelites. Other times, however, as a means of control, they would take the children of Israel captive and ship them out to the various corners of their pagan kingdoms. They did this so that there would not be enough people in any one place to rise up and overthrow the government of their captors.

This latter situation was where Israel found itself in the book of Nehemiah. The nation had been torn apart, and they had lost their national identity. Some individuals loved God and wanted to live for him, but they had become a minority, living among the unbelieving people in the nation who had taken them captive. Nehemiah was one of those who had been taken from his home of Jerusalem, but he rose to a place of prominence in the court of his captor king, where he served as what we might understand to be a chief butler.

In the opening verses of Nehemiah, he received some disturbing news from back home. Apparently, a handful of Jews had fled their captivity and made their way back to Jerusalem. When they arrived, they found that their hometown capital city was in complete ruin: the gates of the city had been burned down and the walls protecting it had been destroyed. When Nehemiah heard this, he became overwhelmed with grief and his heart was burdened for his people.

Nehemiah had the same thought Chad did when his heart was burdened for his fellow warriors: "Someone has to do something about this! Why not me?" Nehemiah prayed God would give him favor with the king as he asked for permission to go to Jerusalem to rebuild the wall to his city. God heard Nehemiah's prayer and not only did the king bless his trip back to Jerusalem to repair the city, but he even gave him all the building materials he needed to make it happen.

As the story unfolds, we see Nehemiah begin to act as both the civil leader of Jerusalem and its general contractor in the rebuilding. He organized the people, got the materials in place, and then he and the people began to build. They did such amazing work that they completed the entire project in just fifty-two days. People observing from the outside commented that the only way the work could have been done so quickly was if it was blessed by God (Nehemiah 6:16). It was an incredible success.

Significantly, however, there were those who didn't like all the good that Nehemiah was doing, even wanting to kill him, but their efforts to destroy him did not move Nehemiah. He had an unfair advantage in knowing the work God had called him to do. When you are focused on fulfilling what God has for you to do, it becomes much easier to ignore the distractions and the opposition. When

you are working on *paying it forward*, you don't have time to focus on anything else.

When the Robichaux family moved from their home in Texas to Westcliffe, Colorado, to start Mighty Oaks, few paid attention. Their plan was simple: tell what God had done in their own family and help others take the same steps. They began to see lives and families restored, and then people who needed hope and healing began to show up in even larger numbers. Before long, a waiting list was growing at a pace that could only be explained (similar to Nehemiah) as a work of God. It was amazing to see and be a part of.

As Mighty Oaks began to grow, people came out of the woodwork to try to tell Chad how he should *really* run it. Some said it was being done wrong; others that it would never last the way he was doing it; some urged that so-called professionals be added to the staff to provide legitimacy; still others warned that the growth must stop because there were not enough financial resources to keep things going.

And there were also those who saw the success of the organization and thought that instead of paying it forward by showing others what God can do, Mighty Oaks needed to diversify and get involved in other things. It's not that other things are bad, but they're not what God put on the hearts of Chad and Kathy. All these people, with all their good suggestions, were trying to keep Chad from rebuilding the wall God intended for him to fix.

Like Nehemiah, Chad kept his focus, stayed the course, and Mighty Oaks has been incredibly blessed by God. Tens of thousands have now been reached through programs for veterans and active-duty service members and their families. Lives have been changed; homes have been put back together; children have been reunited with their parents; chains that bound so many have

been broken; and a genuine freedom, found only in Christ, has been experienced by thousands. All of this has occurred because someone who experienced this healing decided it was his job to pay it forward for others.

Chad is my closest friend, and I am grateful to be able to work alongside him. Weekly, there are still people trying to get him to come off the wall and do something else. But we say, just like Nehemiah did in his day, "I am carrying on a great project and cannot go down. Why should the work stop while I leave it and go down to you?" (Nehemiah 6:3). When we try to pay it forward, there will always be those attempting to distract or divert us, but we will also have an unfair advantage by remembering that God put us here to rebuild this particular part of his wall of restoration, and nothing else is worth coming down off this wall. We have a responsibility to leverage our story so that we can help others. What God has done in our lives, we can't keep to ourselves.

Jeremy M. Stalnecker
Executive Director, Mighty Oaks Foundation;
Author, US Marine Corps Infantry Officer

Resources

WHAT ARE YOU GOING TO DO NOW?

"What shall I do, then,
with Jesus who is called the Messiah?" Pilate asked.

MATTHEW 27:22

Just like Pontius Pilate, when introduced to Jesus, the Roman governor of Judaea asked himself, *What shall I do, then, with Jesus who is called the Messiah?* We all have to answer that question when we learn the truth about Jesus and who he created us to be. Learning truth is one thing, but what you do with that truth is altogether different. It's a choice only you can make. My purpose in writing this book is to share with you the lessons I have learned from both my successes and failures in order to challenge and inspire you to answer that question for yourself and to be all that God created you to be.

It is important that I admit and that you understand that the content in this book alone will not change your life. Will it motivate

and inspire you? I sure hope so! Will it light a fire in your soul to pursue the path and purpose God has for you as a man and a warrior for the kingdom? Well, that is my prayer for you! Yet, the truth is, when you turn the final page and close the cover, you will reengage in life, and the battles you faced before you read this book will still be there. The more you try to change and align your life with God's design for you, the greater the fight will be. You will need to take the motivation you have right now and do something more. You will need to take the next steps.

I could write an entire book on the next steps, but many others already have. There are programs, churches, and (for those in greater need) biblical counseling and mentors to come alongside you in your journey. You don't have to do it alone, and you were never meant to. Remember the chapter "Who's in Your Corner?" It's time for you to get the right cornermen, coaching, and strategies.

Here are the steps to do it:

1. It starts with a relationship with Jesus. You can't be who you're created to be if you don't know the Creator. See Resource #1 for a guide to having a personal relationship with Christ.

2. Find a church home. God created you to be in community with like-minded believers. See Resource #2 for assistance in finding a church home.

3. Learn more and discover what God wants to tell you. You do this through personal prayer and study. There is no substitute for learning and studying God's Word (the Bible), and many great books will take you deeper on your faith journey. See Resource #3A for a recommended reading

list. See Resource #3B for a brief section on why you should believe the Bible.

4. For those of us who have faced trauma and hardships in life, we need others to come alongside and show us the way forward. Free biblical counseling and mentoring is available for everyone. See Resource #5 for more information on biblical counseling.

5. Mighty Oaks Foundation offers free resources, military resiliency conferences, and combat-trauma programs for active duty, veterans, and spouses of the Armed Forces. See Resource #4 for more information on Mighty Oaks and to learn about The Mighty Oaks Journey.

Resource #1

How to Have a Relationship with Jesus Christ

To truly be the man and warrior God created you to be, you must begin a personal relationship with him, for it is only as you align to his will for your life that you can fulfill the purpose for which he created you. Having a relationship with Christ is simply coming to the place where you understand and accept that the Bible is true when it talks about who Jesus is and your need for him as your Savior. There is no magical process needed to enter into a relationship with Christ. However, the following four steps can serve as a guide for anyone who sincerely desires to give his or her life to him.

Recognize Your Condition

In order to find the way to eternal life with God, you must admit you are stuck in sin. (Sin is any act contrary to God's laws and commandments.) Romans 5:12 teaches us that since Adam and Eve (the first man and woman on earth), a sinful nature has been present in all people. Romans 3:23 says, "All have sinned and fall short of the glory of God." The sins you have committed separate you from God and keep you apart from him. But all sin has a penalty—a big one. Romans 6:23 says, "For the wages of sin is death, but the gift of God is eternal life in Christ Jesus our Lord." The "wage" or payment for our sin is spiritual death and eternal separation from God.

Religion and Good Works Are Not the Answers

World religions try to create their own ways to God. Their systems may seem logical, but they cannot bridge the gap created by

our sin or remove the consequences of it. Proverbs 14:12 says, "There is a way that appears to be right, but in the end it leads to death." In other words, our own ideas and opinions are not what matters. God's Word, the Bible, is what provides true answers. It shows us how to receive forgiveness for our sins and wrongdoings and that this forgiveness comes by God's grace—it is his free gift to us. Ephesians 2:8–9 says, "For it is by grace you have been saved, through faith—and that this is not from yourselves, it is the gift of God—not by works, so that no one can boast."

Jesus Christ Provides the Way

Even though you are lost and your sins have separated you from God, he still loves you. In fact, it is *because* he is love that God sent his Son Jesus to be crucified on the cross as a spiritual payment for your sins. John 3:16 explains, "For God so loved the world that he gave his one and only Son, that whoever believes in him shall not perish but have eternal life." Through the death of Jesus, he became the payment for your sins. In Romans 5:8, the Bible says, "God demonstrates his own love for us in this: While we were still sinners, Christ died for us." Through his resurrection three days later, he provided the spiritual power for us to live above the consequences of sin. As a result, we do not have to pay for our sin ourselves. By his grace, salvation—a way out—is provided.

Believe, Repent, and Receive Christ

In order to have a relationship with God and an eternal home with him in heaven, you must stop trusting what you can do (or what any religion says) and must instead place your full trust in Jesus Christ alone for the forgiveness of your sins and for receiving eternal life. Romans 10:13 says, "Everyone who calls on the name of the Lord will be saved." It is a promise directly from God that if you will pray to him, confess that you are a sinner (that is, confess

that you have done things your own way rather than his), ask him to forgive your sins, and turn to him alone to be your Savior, he then promises to spiritually cleanse you, place you in a personal relationship with him, and give you the free gift of eternal life. You can make that decision today by praying to him from your heart. You can pray something like this:

> *God, I know that I am separated from you because of sin. I confess that I cannot save myself. Right now, I turn to you alone to be my Savior. I ask you to save me from the penalty of my sin, and I trust you to provide eternal life to me. I ask that you give me the courage, strength, and direction to be the man and warrior you created me to be. Amen.*

If you have just begun a personal relationship with Christ, I (and others) rejoice with you. Congratulations! You'll never regret this decision! Yet make no mistake, the battle ahead to be a warrior for the kingdom will not be an easy one. So don't attempt to fight alone. Go to Resource #2 for assistance in finding a good church home where you can lock arms with other believers.

Finding a Church Home

Finding the right church home with like-minded believers is an important step in having the accountability and support to live out the new decision you have made. It will not only help you continue to grow spiritually, but you will find strength in numbers. In the right church, you will learn and grow through the teaching of the pastor, and you will have the chance to connect with brothers and even a mentor who will invest in your spiritual growth. You were created to be in community, not to fight alone.

At Mighty Oaks Foundation, we use several resources to find the right church home for the graduates of our programs. Here are a few:

Recommended Web Sources:

9Marks.org/church-search/

TMS.edu/find-a-church/

CalvaryChapel.com/church-locator/

Acts29.com/find-churches/

Recommended Reading

This book represents a starting point in a new journey, not the end of the road. Continue your journey and be intentional about learning more by discovering what God has to tell you personally, through both prayer and personal study. There is no substitute for learning and studying God's Word (the Bible). However, many great books will also take you deeper in your faith journey and will assist and guide you. Below are books we recommend, which we've organized for you by theme.

Spiritual Challenge and Inspiration

The Warrior Soul by Lt. General "Jerry" Boykin and Stu Weber

Tender Warrior by Stu Weber

Wild at Heart by John Eldredge

God's Purpose for Your Life

March or Die by Jeremy Stalnecker

The Purpose Driven Life by Rick Warren

Don't Waste Your Life by John Piper

Spiritual Growth

How to Study the Bible by John MacArthur

Multiply by Francis Chan and Mark Beuving

The Principle of the Path by Andy Stanley

Spiritual Resiliency

The Truth About PTS"D" by Chad Robichaux and Jeremy Stalnecker

Path to Resiliency by Chad Robichaux and Jeremy Stalnecker

Resilient Warriors by Major General Robert Dees

Marriage and Family

Marriage Advance by Chad and Kathy Robichaux

Marriage on the Rock by Jimmy Evans

Love Is a Decision by Dr. Gary Smalley

Addictions

The Heart of Addiction by Mark E. Shaw

Addictions—A Banquet in the Grave by Edward T. Welch

The Bondage Breaker by Neil T. Anderson

Why Believe the Bible

There are many reasons why you should choose to believe the Bible over other religious books. I am a skeptic by nature, so the study of whether there is evidence to support the Christian faith (this study is called apologetics) is one that fascinates me. The more I study it, the more it has built my confidence in the Bible.

One of my favorite apologetics teachers is Dr. Voddie Baucham, who said, "I choose to believe the Bible because it is a reliable collection of historical documents written down by eyewitnesses during the lifetime of other eyewitnesses. They report of supernatural events that took place in fulfillment of specific prophecies and claimed that their writings are Divine rather than human in origin." I highly encourage you to watch the online sermon "Why I Choose to Believe the Bible" by Dr. Voddie Baucham.

Some great books on apologetics include:

Expository Apologetics by Dr. Voddie Baucham

A New Kind of Apologist by Sean McDowell

The Case for Christ by Lee Strobel

Resource #4

Biblical Counseling

Many of us have faced trauma and hardships in life, and we need others to come alongside us and show us the way forward. Biblical counseling is the best way to do this. Biblical counseling means that the counselor believes and counsels from a perspective that uses the wisdom found in God's Word to lead people to hope, restoration, and new purpose. Biblical counseling is typically available at no cost, and we at Mighty Oaks Foundation have found great success by connecting military warriors and family members to biblical counselors nationwide through our partnership with the Biblical Counseling Coalition.

If you're looking for resources relating to biblical counseling or if you want to locate a biblical counselor in your local area, the Biblical Counseling Coalition is great resource. For more information visit BiblicalCounselingCoalition.org.

Resource #5

Mighty Oaks Warrior Programs

Mighty Oaks Foundation offers free conferences for military commands on spiritual resiliency and free resiliency and combat-trauma programs for active-duty members, veterans, and spouses of the Armed Forces.

Legacy Program for Men

Our six-day intensive peer-to-peer program serves as the catalyst to help warriors discover the answers to the big questions in life. Challenges related to the struggles of daily military life, combat deployments, and the symptoms of post-traumatic stress (PTS) surface during these six days, and the Legacy Program for Men teaches how to fight through these challenges, which might have been limiting their personal success.

Legacy Program for Women

The Legacy Program for Women is a process of learning to become a Virtuous Woman—"The Proverbs 31" woman. This three-day retreat leads spouses and military women through a time of learning, exploration, and growth with an aim to cultivate virtuous characteristics in a safe, open, and nurturing environment.

Marriage Advance

Our three-day Marriage Advance conferences are designed for couples to gain a better understanding of the struggles they face and how to advance their relationships into the marriage God intended. We structure conversations around needs, expectations, goals, and forgiveness to help couples move forward.

Military Resiliency Programs

We believe that resiliency is comprised of three pillars: mind, body, and spirit. Our Military Resiliency Programs are designed to properly equip our nation's warriors on the front end of conflict so they and their families can have a true resiliency and a mindset that is preventative of the hardships that many of them face.

These programs are available at no cost to our Warriors. To support them and learn more, please visit MightyOaksPrograms.org

ACKNOWLEDGMENTS

I am so grateful to the many people whom God has brought alongside me who have been key in the development of this book. They include:

The warriors I have had the privilege to serve with, both at home and abroad. I am honored to share glimpses into our stories in an effort to bring hope and inspiration to others.

My family, who endured my preoccupation throughout the writing of this book as I was engaged in prayer, thought, and long hours. They understand better than anyone why the message of *An Unfair Advantage* is so important for me to share. They have personally experienced both my best and my worst but love me anyway and continue to believe in me. I am forever indebted to my incredible wife, Kathy, who, when I was at rock bottom, challenged me to fight for the things that are most important in life. Demonstrating her own willingness to fight when all seemed hopeless, she is one of the greatest warriors I have ever known. I am also grateful to my three amazing children, who have always been worth fighting for. I thank God every day for choosing me to be their dad!

My mentor and friend, Steve Toth, who showed me the way forward and encouraged me to pay it forward. Words will never convey my eternal gratitude.

My team at Mighty Oaks Foundation—my true brothers whom God has blessed me with! These are the guys who I get to share life with, and I thank them for making it possible for me to have the bandwidth to accomplish a project of this magnitude.

And to all those who offered input, read, wrote, inspired, and assisted me in bringing this book to life, I thank you!

Much credit for taking this book from a thought to a reality goes to John Mizerak. He managed the project, pushed me to meet deadlines, and challenged me to dig deeper to be able to share what God did in my life.

I am especially grateful for my good friend David Barton, whom I deeply respect and admire. He went above and beyond, using his experience, gifts, and talents to help me organize the book in a way that will best communicate to those on whom (we pray) *An Unfair Advantage* will have an eternal impact.

Most important, I thank God! It's because of his love, his grace, and how he uniquely created me as a warrior with a special purpose that I am able to be part of the great battle for the hearts and souls of men.

ABOUT THE AUTHOR

CHAD M. ROBICHAUX, BCPC, MBA

Chad is a former Force Recon marine and DoD contractor with eight deployments to Afghanistan as part of a Joint Special Operations Command (JSOC) Task Force. After overcoming his personal battles with PTSD and nearly becoming a veteran suicide statistic, Chad founded the Mighty Oaks Foundation, a leading nonprofit, serving the active duty and military veteran communities with highly successful faith-based combat trauma and resiliency programs. Having spoken to over 150,000 active-duty troops and led life-saving programs for over 3,800 active military and veterans at four Mighty Oaks Ranches around the nation, Chad has become a go-to resource and is considered a subject matter expert on faith-based solutions to PTSD, having advised the Trump administration, Congress, the VA, and the highest levels of the DoD. Currently, Chad serves as the chairman for the Faith Based Veterans Service Alliance (FBVSA) collaborating with the White House on behalf of a coalition of faith-based Veteran Service Organizations, and is a surrogate speaker and national board member for Veterans Coalition for Trump.

Chad has written five books related to veteran care, donat-

ing over 100,000 copies to the troops during his resiliency speaking tours. He is regularly featured on national media, such as Fox News, OANN, The O'Reilly Factor, The Blaze, TBN, The 700 Club, USA Today and has appeared in a short film by I Am Second. Currently, a life-story motion picture is being produced based on the stories in this book.

In addition to Chad's military service, he is a former federal agent and law enforcement officer who was awarded the Medal of Valor for bravery. Chad is married to his wife, Kathy, and they have a daughter and two sons. Hunter is a third-generation Marine Combat veteran in the Robichaux family. Chad and his two sons are lifelong martial artists. Chad is a third degree Brazilian jiu-jitsu black belt under Carlson Gracie Jr. and is a former Professional Mixed Martial Arts Champion, having competed at the highest levels of the sport.

THE MIGHTY OAKS JOURNEY

When Chad Robichaux realized that countless other combat veterans face the same psychological, emotional, and spiritual challenges he did after his service in Afghanistan (challenges causing some twenty-plus suicides a day and staggering divorce rates among military families), Chad wondered, *Why doesn't someone do something about this?* He eventually realized that the answer was *Why not me?* and so began Mighty Oaks.

It is a story of God's transformational power to turn tragedy into triumph. It is a journey starting with one man's brokenness from war, one woman's willingness to fight for her family, and their faith in God's promise from Isaiah 61:3 that we can rise from the ashes and become mighty oaks of righteousness.

Many great men stepped in to mentor Chad and Kathy past their struggles, but none more than Steve Toth and Pastor Jeff Wells of WoodsEdge Community Church. It was through this church that Chad and Kathy were later ordained and commissioned as ministers and sent to begin the Mighty Oaks ministry to America's military warriors and families.

The first programs for men were launched in Westcliffe, Colorado, with non-active duty veterans. Chad and Kathy served alongside the Dave Roever Foundation for more than a year while developing the methodology that would become Mighty Oaks Warrior Programs (MOWP).

MOWP uses a grassroots approach, empowering veterans to begin their healing and then be a positive impact on those around them. Those warriors, challenged by this peer-to-peer model, rose to meet the challenge and found hope and purpose beyond their military service, grabbing hold of a future worth living

again. As they left the programs, they sent their brothers, which made the program grow rapidly, especially with warriors coming from US Marine Corps Wounded Warrior Battalion West, which housed a large population of Marine Corps combat veterans.

During this time of growth and increasing demand, Dave Roever introduced Chad to Wayne Hughes Jr. to explore the possibility of taking Mighty Oaks to El Paso de Robles, California. (Interestingly, *El Paso de Robles* translates to "The Path of the Oaks." We at Mighty Oaks say this was definitely a God wink!) Wayne, a very successful businessman, had previously launched Serving California, a nonprofit philanthropy arm for his many companies.

It was in Wayne's heart to see the Lord's hand over our returning American warriors, and he wanted to run a veterans' program at his ranch. He allowed MOWP to do so on the condition that if he liked the program, he'd build a lodge there to host it. He did like it, especially its results.

A partnership between Mighty Oaks and Serving California took root, and SkyRose Lodge was built. This became the primary home of Mighty Oaks Warrior Programs. However, the rapidly increasing influx of warriors and military families has resulted (so far) in three other regional locations: Blaylock Ranch in Junction, Texas, Warrior Retreat at Bull Run in Haymarket, Virginia, and The Wilds in Columbus, Ohio.

As our work continues with veterans and spouses, we receive active-duty warriors on official orders from the various branches. We also have become a top resource for the US military, having trained and equipped more than one hundred thousand warriors in combat readiness through Resiliency Conferences at bases across the country. This included Chad and Jeremy authoring *The Path to Resiliency*, a spiritual-resiliency book used as a free resource for the US military.

Even though Mighty Oaks Warrior Programs has expanded in both numbers and geographic locations, our vision remains the same: to assist our nation's warriors and families by challenging, equipping, and empowering them to take the help they receive and spread it to those in their own circles of influence. We now have more than fifteen hundred Mighty Oaks alumni, and we take great pride in not having lost one to suicide to date. Beyond each warrior's healing he is challenged, equipped, and empowered to care for his brothers, bringing both a solution to the problem and a purpose for those willing to share that solution with others.

Together, we can all strive toward the common goal of ending the war at home by finding a hope and a future and aligning with the purpose for which God created us. We will continue to lead others to fulfill the promise of Isaiah 61:3: to rise from the ashes and become mighty oaks!

Fully paid scholarships are available for all MOWP for active-duty or veteran military personnel, as well as their spouses, by applying online. For more information on programs, or on how you can participate in donating or supporting MOWP, visit:

www.MightyOaksPrograms.org

AN UNFAIR ADVANTAGE

10-Part Study Guide
A Journey to Restoration & Purpose

By Chad M. Robichaux and Jamison S. Warner

Contents

Instructions

We have developed a simple, effective process for utilizing and maximizing the resources available from *An Unfair Advantage*. Thank you to Mighty Oaks Foundation for developing a video course to accompany this study guide and help lead you on your journey to restoration, purpose, and becoming the man and warrior who God created you to be.

The lessons in the videos and the study guide are founded on the same principles and teachings of the Mighty Oaks Warrior Programs attended by thousands of our nation's warriors each year.

Follow this simple outline to get started:

- Begin by completing Session 1, which includes assigned readings from *An Unfair Advantage* and questions for reflection.
- Next, visit MightyOaksPrograms.org/AUA-Course and enter password: AUA2021 to access exclusive video content discussions. Watch these by yourself, with a friend or two, or as a group.
- Gather with your small group and engage in a discussion of what you've learned from the videos and the study guide.
- Repeat the steps above for Sessions 2–10.

Trauma Is Not a Combat Issue; It's a Life Issue

So much attention has been given to the PTSD and suicide epidemic in the veteran community in recent years and rightly so. The number of PTSD diagnoses among those who have served in our Armed Forces is at an unprecedented level, and veterans and active duty service members are taking their own lives at a tragic rate. As General Boykin stated in the foreword, "Chad Robichaux is one of those combat warriors who came home from war and struggled with the aftermath of his experiences. His marriage was in serious trouble, as were his relationships with others he cared about. Chad was not willing to accept that there was any enemy he could not defeat, especially one so ill-defined as PTSD." Much has been and continues to be done to help combat horrific events like Chad's and countless others. And yet, as terrible as these statistics are, veterans and active service members are not the only ones suffering from the effects of trauma.

All of us will deal with trauma at some point in our lives. It's a fallen, sinful world, and trauma is part of that reality. We are all in a battle whether we acknowledge it or not. An enemy is trying to destroy you and your legacy. Struggle, disappointment, pain, and regret are all part of the package deal. Chad learned this first-hand. "But he finally found an enemy that he could not overcome by just being stronger, faster, and tougher than the adversary," continued Boykin. "This time he was losing his match, and it was the most important one of his life with everything he cared about at stake. He tried everything he knew, but he was failing. There just had to be more…"And there was."

Amidst the battles of life are also peace, joy, purpose, and hope. How do some people, like Chad, seem to come out the

other side of traumatic experiences and actually flourish? How can we get hold of that hope? Was it something in his training or his DNA? Join Chad on his journey of discovering the unfair advantage available to everyone, whether Special Forces, military, first responder, businessman, husband, father, student…anyone.

This unfair advantage is simple, but it's not easy. Is the journey worth the work? Read on to discover for yourself. There's no better time to get in the fight.

Rules of Engagement

The sessions that follow are designed to enhance your reading of *An Unfair Advantage* and help you engage with the concepts and lessons throughout the book on a more personal level. This guide can be completed independently but works best in a small group setting where participants can share ideas, experiences, and wisdom. As with all battles, rules of engagement help secure victory in the fight. Here are some "rules" to keep in mind:

1. **Cultivate conversation.** Small groups are most effective when members share. Everyone needs to participate. Decide now, as a group, that you will establish a confidential, authentic environment. Go deep so that you all go the distance.

2. **The study questions and fill-in-the-blanks help you engage with the material and your group.** Free-flowing, spontaneous discussion and sharing will yield greater results and understanding of the material and yourself, so be at liberty to dive deeper into areas that need more exploration.

3. **Stay on mission**. The more conversation, the better—but avoid straying too far from your objectives. Help each other stay on point and be ready to politely refocus the discussion when necessary.

The first section in each session, GET READY, provides the chapter(s) to read from the book that correspond with the session. Read these chapters beforehand and then use the questions and writings found in the GET FOCUSED section to prepare your mind for discussion.

The next section, GET IN THE FIGHT, will help you apply the

lessons that Chad presents to your personal life and your growth. You are encouraged to answer all the questions honestly and transparently. These are powerful weapons in the fight for authentic manhood.

Once you finish answering the questions and engaging in discussion, the Get Recalibrated section offers a short summary of the main ideas of that session. Lastly, the Get Prepared section contains your marching orders for the next session.

TRY SOMETHING DIFFERENT

Get Ready

Read the following:

- Introduction
- Chapter 1: The Killing Pool

Get Focused

Have you ever felt like there must be something more, a greater purpose to this life you're living?

Get in the Fight

1. In the Introduction, Chad talks about a yearning, a restlessness with which many of us can relate. In what ways do you identify with this sense of being out of place?

2. Chad claims that gaining his unfair advantage came from asking himself this question: If what you are doing isn't working, then why not try something different?

a. Make a short list of substitutions you tried or used in order to fill that void:

   - _____
   - _____
   - _____

   b. What was still missing or what part(s) of that void were still present after each substitution?

   c. What do you risk losing by beginning this study with an open mind and a willingness to try something different?

   d. What could you possibly gain?

   e. What do you risk losing if you choose not to change?

3. Chad vividly describes some of the atrocities the Taliban committed against the Afghan people. He gives us a glimpse into how that knowledge replaced his patriotism with hate-fueled vengeance. Though his hardening of his heart was born of a righteous indignation, how can the application of the chapter's opening verse, "Above all else, guard your heart, for everything you do flows from it" (Proverbs 4:23), help us in situations where we have dropped our guard?

4. Discuss circumstances in which you allowed your situation to pull you further away from God instead of letting the events draw you closer to him.

5. Chad comments that he would often tell his wife how God could not be in such an evil place as Afghanistan. He later comes to realize that what he describes as "the absence of God" was actually "the tangible presence of evil." Instead of leaning into God in the midst of this evil, he allowed hate to fill his heart, leading him to conclude he could not be a Christian. He could not reconcile how to be a Christian man, a man of morality, and an effective warrior at the same time. Describe a time in your life when you felt you couldn't be a Christian because of your circumstances or season of life, during which you effectively put God on a shelf. What filled the void in your heart while God was on the shelf?

6. When discussing what a man of righteousness looks and acts like, two extremes exist within our current culture, which has gone to great lengths to emasculate men and the principles of manhood. On one extreme, masculinity is seen as a great and oppressive evil. The other extreme assumes that a man who stands against evil must be driven by fear, hate, rage, and vengeance. Both of these perceptions are wrong and create a false imprisonment. Describe a time in your life when you were falsely imprisoned because you allowed fear, hate, rage, vengeance, selfishness, or societal expectations to fuel your passions and drive your actions.

Read Ephesians 6:10–18 in your Bible or on your device.
- What enemies do we engage with in battle as described in verses 10–12?

- What various pieces of armor are listed in verses 13–18? Is this armor adequate to safeguard your life during battle?

- How can the spiritual armor described in Ephesians 6:10–18 give you an unfair advantage on your battlefield? Be specific.

Spend time praying with your group. Ask God to help all of you draw closer to him and to rely on his truths and promises in times of difficulty.

Get Recalibrated

No matter the circumstances, if we align our lives with the life God created us to live, and if we walk onto the battlefields of life wearing the full armor of God, then we will have an unfair advantage and find victory in the midst of battle.

Get Prepared

To prepare for the next session's reflection and discussion, read Chapters 2 and 3.

PRESS FORWARD AND LEAD

Get Ready

Read the following:

- Chapter 2: Getting off the X
- Chapter 3: Valley of the Shadow of Death

Get Focused

Have you ever found yourself "standing on the X," unsure of your next move and looking for someone to lead you to safety?

Get in the Fight

1. Chad discusses how we often find ourselves in a position where the going gets tough and how we tend to choose the "known and bad" over the "unknown and new." Sometimes we move toward the freedom found in the promises of God but then return to the bondage of familiarity. Discuss a time in your life when you intentionally chose the known and bad over the unknown and new.

2. Chapter 2 closes with a reminder that we will all find ourselves on the X at some point in our lives, probably more than once. We have the power to choose what to do in those situations: stay on the X and get dragged back to where we came from (or worse, stay there and die), or recognize that we are on the X and press forward toward God's promised victory: "'For I know the plans I have for you,' declares the Lord, 'plans to prosper you and not to harm you, plans to give you hope and a future'" (Jeremiah 29:11). Name specific ways in which you can move forward with a firm reliance on God. Keeping Jeremiah 29:11 in mind, what does that look like?

When difficulties arise, do you feel alone in your distress? All too often, our difficult circumstances and experiences seem impossible for others to understand, and we buy into the lie that we are alone. We become self-focused. Yet as Chad points out, while the people, places, and timing of your circumstances may be unique, the reality is that many of the people around us face similar challenges, like when Chad and his companions found a way over the rubble in the road. In every situation, someone must go first. There must be a leader.

3. What keeps you from taking the lead?

To lead is an opportunity to step into the unknown and new. It's an act of obedience. We won't always understand why we are in the position to lead, but when we lead out of obedience, others will follow. Some steps of obedience are easy, maybe even comfortable, but others feel as though we're stepping off a cliff, blindly

trusting that our next step will land on solid, level ground. But if we trust that God has put us in a position to lead and trust him, and if we are willing to take a step of faith, then it can lead to the victory that only comes from a life of following God.

4. Share a situation in which you felt alone and uncertain of the outcome, so you retreated to the known and the bad. How could that situation have ended differently if you had moved forward in faith instead of staying on the X?

5. What pre-decisions can you make to increase the likelihood that you will move forward the next time you find yourself on the X?

6. Discuss ways in which you can embrace the role of leader in your sphere of influence.

7. Discuss circumstances in which it is more effective to follow someone else's lead. How can you specifically enhance their leadership by following them?

Spend time in your group praying for each other to recognize when you find yourself on the X and to have the courage to move forward and lead others when necessary.

Get Recalibrated

Engaging in the battles of life will find us on the X more often than we like. Recognizing when you are on the X allows you the opportunity to move forward and trust God's "plans to prosper you and not to harm you, plans to give you hope and a future" (Jeremiah 29:11). When you move forward in obedience, you might be surprised to find that others in similar circumstances are following you.

Get Prepared

To prepare for the next session's reflection and discussion, read Chapters 4 and 5.

FIGHT FOR YOUR PURPOSE

Get Ready

Read the following:

- Chapter 4: The Girl on Chicken Street
- Chapter 5: Created for a Purpose

Get Focused

Have you ever wondered why bad things happen to good people, or why good things seem to happen to bad people?

Get in the Fight

Adversity seems to be an ever-present travel companion on the journey of life. Have you ever wondered why our first reaction is so often to blame God when adversity strikes? How does that make sense when we know truths such as these:

- "God is love" (1 John 4:8).
- "God is light, and in him there is no darkness at all" (1 John 1:5 NKJV).
- "Every good gift and perfect gift is from above, and comes down from the Father of lights, with whom there is no variation or shadow of turning" (James 1:17 NKJV).

- "Gracious is the Lord, and righteous; yes, our God is merciful" (Psalm 116:5 NKJV).

When we are struggling, our tendency is to question God's love for us because we don't understand why he'd allow bad things to happen. Where's the love, right? In his book *Trusting God: Even When Life Hurts*, author Jerry Bridges explains it this way:

> When we begin to question the love of God, we need to remember who we are. We have absolutely no claim on His love. We don't deserve one bit of God's goodness to us. ... Any time that we are tempted to doubt God's love for us, we should go back to the Cross. We should reason somewhat in this fashion: If God loved me enough to give His Son to die for me when I was His enemy, surely He loves me enough to care for me now that I am His child. Having loved me to the ultimate extent at the Cross, He cannot possibly fail to love me in my times of adversity. Having given such a priceless gift as His Son, surely He will also give all else that is consistent with His glory and my good.[1]

1. When bad things happen, whether to you or others, who do you tend to blame?

2. Why do you think God allows us to experience adversity?

3. According to Bridges, "Our suffering has meaning and purpose in God's eternal plan, and He brings or allows to come into our lives only that which is for His glory and our good." How should that understanding change our perspective on adversity?

Chad refers to the story of Joseph in Chapter 5. Like most of us navigating the storms of life, Joseph experienced rejection, fear, confusion, and hopelessness, yet somehow, in the midst of all his suffering, he maintained his integrity, obedience, and faithfulness.

4. What was Joseph's "secret" that saw him through so many years of hardship?

5. Discuss how the application of Joseph's "secret" to your hardships may affect not only your outlook but also your outcome.

Following Christ does not guarantee a life free of trouble. Quite the opposite, especially when you consider Jesus's words in Luke 9:23–24: "If anyone would come after me, let him deny himself and take up his cross daily and follow me. For whoever would save his life will lose it, but whoever loses his life for my sake will save it" (ESV). Like Chad's illustration of the butterfly struggling to emerge from its cocoon, the struggle is a necessary part of the process in becoming who we were created to be.

6. What do you stand to gain by aligning your life with the one God created for you?

7. If God created you for a purpose, then how would living within that purpose change your perspective of life?

Remember that "suffering produces perseverance; perseverance, character; and character, hope" (Romans 5:3–4). Hope in what? Well, as Chad explained, there is value in struggles, but you may have to wait until you're on the other side to understand how those struggles helped you become who you were born to be.

8. What purposes were you created for?

Spend time in your group praying for each other to live as leaders and warriors and to lead well during times of battle.

Get Recalibrated

God created each of us to be leaders and warriors. Whom we lead and the battles we face are specific to our unique circumstances and places in life. We all have the choice: either lie down and let life and others step on us, or stand up and fight for what is right and be that example, that leader, to those within our sphere of influence.

Get Prepared

To prepare for the next session's reflection and discussion, read Chapters 7 and 11.

BROTHERHOOD

Get Ready

Read the following:

- Chapter 7: The Captain of the *Titanic*
- Chapter 11: Who's in Your Corner?

Get Focused

Isolation can lead to a distorted view of the world and ourselves.

Get in the Fight

1. Anyone who has spent any length of time here on earth has experienced some degree of hurt or trauma. They're natural consequences of the sinful nature of this world: "I have said these things to you, that in me you may have peace. In the world you will have tribulation. But take heart; I have overcome the world" (John 16:33 ESV). Discuss a time in your life when you felt overwhelmed by your circumstances and without peace. How did you deal with discomfort?

2. Did you or could you have turned to someone for help, advice, or accountability? If so, who?

3. Name fights, battles, or struggles you've faced.

4. Did you have someone in your corner? If so, who?

This session is about having brotherhood—like-minded men—in your corner of life to help you navigate dark times. When you have the right kind of people in your life, you can find levity, laughter, and even joy in the midst of tragedy.

5. Have you ever encountered someone who, while in the midst of trauma, pain, or tragedy, was somehow able to stand tall under the weight of it all? Why do you think they remained unbroken despite their circumstances?

6. How does having an eternal perspective change the way we look at trials?

7. Why is accountability so important during times of trial?

8. How can finding joy during your trials help others in their troubles?

Spend time in your group praying for each other to develop authentic relationships with like-minded men. Pray that God would reveal cornermen for you to fight alongside.

Get Recalibrated

Circumstances have a tendency to go from bad to worse when we allow ourselves to isolate from like-minded men who will hold us accountable and encourage us. When you begin to struggle, take that first step toward victory by picking up the phone and calling your cornermen.

Get Prepared

To prepare for the next session's reflection and discussion, read Chapters 6 and 8.

ANGER

Get Ready

Read the following:

- Chapter 6: You Killed Me
- Chapter 8: Out of Control

Get Focused

We live in a sinful, fallen world. Anger is something we all deal with, but it's what is in your heart that determines how you respond to that anger.

Get in the Fight

Imagine yourself driving down a highway, cruising at a good clip and tapping on the steering wheel to the beat of the song coming through your speakers. Suddenly, a person who clearly should have forfeited his driver's license years ago merges onto the highway directly in front of you, traveling at a speed that only your great-grandmother would be proud of. You can't swerve into the lane beside you without colliding into an unsuspecting motorist, so you slam on the brake pedal and pound the horn through your

steering wheel, all the while resisting the urge to let that driver know how you think he's number one.

1. We all deal with our anger. For some of us, it's on a daily basis. What things really tick you off? What pet peeves set you on edge, leaving you wanting to lash out?

2. According to Chapter 8, how does Jesus respond to situations that make him mad?

3. How is he able to maintain control of his anger in those situations? Look up the following verses (we used the NKJV) and fill in the blanks.

Ecclesiastes 7:9

Do not hasten in your _____ to be _____, for anger rests in the _____ of _____.

Proverbs 29:11

A fool _____ _____ his feelings, but a _____ _____ holds them back.

James 1:20

For the _____ of man does not produce the _____ of _____.

Proverbs 14:29

He who is _____ to _____ has great understanding, but he who is _____ exalts folly.

_____ from _____, and _____ wrath; Do not _____—it only causes _____.

4. What do these verses tell us about anger?

5. It can feel so good to vent our anger, but what do these Bible verses tell us?

- Ephesians 4:26
- James 1:20
- Ephesians 4:31
- Proverbs 19:11
- Proverbs 15:1

6. Thinking about the stories Chad shared and how Jesus dealt with anger, what should our response to anger be?

7. As Chad mentioned, the great theologian Uncle Ben of Marvel's *Spider-Man* says, "With great power comes great responsibility."[2] According to what Chad shared in the chapter, what is that responsibility?

8. How can brotherhood help us exercise that responsibility?

Spend some time in your group praying for each other to keep your anger in check through an authentic brotherhood.

Get Recalibrated

Anger is a God-given emotion that is appropriate in the proper time and place. Be angry about the things that make God angry and be in control of your anger at all other times. Use your brotherhood of authentic, godly relationships to hold your anger accountable.

Get Prepared

To prepare for the next session's reflection and discussion, read Chapters 9 and 10.

KEEP THE END IN MIND

Get Ready

Read the following:

- Chapter 9: Trading My Birthright
- Chapter 10: Not the Solution

Get Focused

These chapters share stories related to fighting. Fighting for marriages, family, and a lasting, positive legacy. Chad and Kathy's story was one of success, whereas Pete and Heather's story was tragic. Still, each person in both stories will leave a legacy one day. Each of us must decide what kind of legacy we want to leave and ask ourselves if we are willing to fight the difficult fight to make it happen.

Get in the Fight

Brazilian jiu-jitsu master Renzo Gracie said, "People often see fighting as an ugly thing that denigrates the human being. In reality, you see fighting in everything, no matter what it is. Upon waking up in the morning, getting out of bed is a fight, believe it. So, the will to fight is actually the best thing a man can have in his soul."[3]

1. In what contexts do you see fighting?

2. How can the will to fight be one of the best things for a man to have in his soul?

3. How can this fighting spirit be detrimental?

Chad observes that his downward spiral wasn't a direct result of incidents of his life; rather, it was a result of how he chose to respond to those incidents—how he coped and sought comfort. He remarks that brokenness leaves a hole in the heart, and what you attempt to fill that hole with makes all the difference. As Chad explains, chasing and catching the false god of success was not only unfulfilling but also a temporary fix that allowed the void to grow.

4. What "gods" have you chased in an attempt to fill the hole in your heart?

5. Thinking about his square-peg-in-a-round-hole analogy, what is the only true solution to a God-shaped hole in your heart?

6. Why is it so easy to see these holes in the hearts of others but not our own?

7. In what areas of your life have you seen a slow destruction and dismantling of your peace and purpose?

In the story of Jacob and Esau, we see Esau make decisions based on temporary feelings and circumstances. He is not living with the end in mind. He forsakes his legacy and his potential impact on future generations for an immediate albeit temporary solution to an intense emotion.

8. How can we safeguard our legacies and our potential impact on future generations from temporary solutions to current discomforts?

9. Why is living with the end in mind so important?

All of us will leave a legacy. That's not an option; it's beyond your control. But what kind of legacy you leave for those who come after you is absolutely within your control.

10. Discuss what you want your legacy to look like. Be as specific as you can.

11. Write down at least three traits you'd like your legacy to be characterized by:

1. _____
2. _____
3. _____

12. What specific actions or behaviors do you need to change in order for these three traits to be realized?

1. _____
2. _____
3. _____

13. Name specific actions you take or behaviors you perform that you must continue in order for the three traits to become true of your legacy.

1. _____
2. _____
3. _____

14. Job said, "Shall we accept good from God, and not trouble?" If we live with the end in mind and recognize that God is sovereign, then we, too, will see as Job did. How might you apply Job's question to your circumstances in order to help you press on through times of trouble?

15. When we diet or exercise, we don't expect positive, easy results. So why do we expect immediate, positive results and no struggles when we fight for something meaningful?

16. How can we prepare for the inevitable struggles we will face?

17. How can we press on toward the goal that God calls us to pursue?

Spend time in your group praying for each other to have the moral courage to live with the end in mind and to implement these changes in your life on a daily basis.

Get Recalibrated

It's been said that your legacy is like planting seeds in a garden for plants that you will never see. Live with the end in mind. We don't know how much time we have on earth, but it's not the amount that is important; it's what we do with the time we are given that matters. Consider the time you have remaining as a gift to leave the next generation. Commit to living the rest of your life as an authentic man of God. Leave a legacy that your loved ones will be proud and eager to emulate.

Get Prepared

To prepare for the next session's reflection and discussion, read Chapters 12 and 13.

FIGHT TO WIN

Get Ready

Read the following:

- Chapter 12: A Pre-Decision to Win
- Chapter 13: A Time to Fight

Get Focused

Physical preparation for the challenges you will face is wise, but it's not enough. You must also be mentally prepared. More often than not, your mental preparedness will play a much more important role in the battles you fight. We must first decide that the victory will be worth the fight, and when we do fight, we must fight to win.

Get in the Fight

In so many areas of work and play, we plan, train, and fight to win. And yet, when it comes to the battles in life, we often fail to plan, train, or win. We let life's battles sneak up on us, as if we didn't foresee them, and they blindside us. The truth is that you can anticipate these battles. You can study your enemy and anticipate his attacks. You can have an unfair advantage and

make a pre-decision to win. Think ahead of the battles that lie ahead of you.

1. Chad says if we are going to be the men God calls us to be, we must be willing to fight but also have discernment over which battles to engage in.

   a. What are some of the battles, both physical and spiritual, that you know you will face?

   b. If there is a time for everything, how do we determine whether it is a time to fight?

2. We are in a spiritual war against evil—against Satan. How can you study your enemy and anticipate his attacks?

3. What can you do in advance to ensure your victory?

4. Pick a battle you face and talk through a visualization of your victory.

According to Chad, the best thing you can do to prepare for life's battles is to intentionally align your will with God's. He explains that his ultimate motivation for winning his fight with Joseph Sandoval was to get his hands on the microphone so that he could share the mission of Mighty Oaks and God.

5. How does aligning our will and our lives with God's give us an unfair advantage?

   a. When our goal is to give glory to God, he will often put us in situations that seem impossible to win. What should our response to these kinds of circumstances be?

   b. How do situations like this glorify him?

6. How can we exercise an unfair advantage and win the war by knowing when to fight boldly and when to remain patient, waiting for the opportunity to engage in the bigger battles?

Spend time in your group praying for each other to have the wisdom and discernment to engage your battles in ways that honor God.

Get Recalibrated

In these against-all-odds scenarios, we can do what we can, and then we have to trust that God will do what only he can do. God loves to use the unexpected to do the unimaginable. Why? Because it points us towards him. It reminds us that true victory comes from his hand, and you cannot lose if you are following his lead.

Get Prepared

To prepare for the next session's reflection and discussion, read Chapter 14.

LEAVE A LEGACY

Get Ready

Read the following:

- Chapter 14: A Warrior's Legacy

Get Focused

Being a man is so much more than a momentary, earthly conquest. No single act in life transitions us into manhood, but there is a defining moment. We were not created to be consumers; rather, we are designed to produce. We are innately designed to serve and produce for others and the world around us. As authentic men of God, we have the ability to leave a legacy that will be cherished, emulated, and passed down to future generations. But first, we must become men.

Get in the Fight

Let's begin by challenging our old ways of thinking about manhood. Chad discusses the misperception that manhood comes from a momentary act, such as getting your first job, turning eighteen, having sex for the first time, or winning your first fight. If

these assumptions are incorrect, then we must start by asking the most basic question about manhood.

1. What defines a man?

2. Now that we understand what defines a man, let's see how you measure up. Are you a man?

We often equate manhood with courage—physical courage, specifically. Warriors on the battlefield are often seen as men, and their heroism inspires us. Like the quote from Billy Graham that Chad cites: "Courage is contagious. When a brave man takes a stand, the spines of others are often stiffened."[4] But have you ever truly defined courage?

3. Define courage.

4. What is the most courageous thing you've ever done?

5. Define a coward.

6. Name a current challenge that you face that you initially feared to take on because it was too difficult or intimidating?

7. Define passivity.

8. What does a passive man look like?

Leaving a legacy worth passing on to the next generation does not happen on its own, nor will it be the path of least resistance. The only person capable of creating your legacy as one worthy of the generations to follow is you, but you have to be willing to put in the work.

Spend time in your group praying for each other to reject passivity and lead courageously as authentic men of God.

Get Recalibrated
Living your life as an authentic man of God will require a lot of you. You must reject passivity, continue to move forward even when the going gets tough, and lead courageously. The health of the next generation is depending on you!

Get Prepared
To prepare for the next session's reflection and discussion, read Chapter 15.

COURAGE IN TIMES OF PERSECUTION

Get Ready

Read the following:

- Chapter 15: The Good Fight

Get Focused

Every one of us has found himself, at some point, in a situation that called for some amount of courage. Sometimes, physical courage is called for, while other times require moral courage. We tend to equate having enough courage with overcoming a situation, but some circumstances call for the courage to stay silent or even back down in humility. A correct response will always require a combination of courage and wisdom.

Get in the Fight

After telling the story of his encounter with the hotheaded tribal lady, Chad writes, "There are times to be courageous and bold, and there are times to be humble and refrain from fighting until another day. There will also be times when we fight and fail, or even when we fail to try at all."

1. How can we determine the correct response in any given situation?

   a. What criteria do you use to decide whether you fight, submit, or withdraw?

   b. How will aligning your life to God's design help you discern the correct course of action?

2. How can fighting and failing yield positive results?

   a. We are told that when we align our life to God's, we may fail, but we won't be defeated. What is the difference between failure and defeat?

   b. How can this understanding shape your perspective of current and future trials and challenges?

3. Name two current social topics that everybody is talking about in the media.

   a. What does the Bible say about these topics?

   b. What does mainstream America think of these biblical views?

4. Let's look at John 15:18–20: "If the world hates you, you know that it hated Me before *it hated* you. If you were of the world, the world would love its own. Yet because you are not of the world, but I chose you out of the world, therefore the world hates you. Remember the word that I said to you, 'A servant is not greater than his master.' If they persecuted Me, they will also persecute you. If they kept My word, they will keep yours also" (NKJV).

    a. "If the world hates you, you know that it hated Me before *it hated* you" (v. 18). Why is the world so against Jesus and his mission?

    b. "If you were of the world, the world would love its own. Yet because you are not of the world, but I chose you out of the world, therefore the world hates you" (v. 19). This verse tells us we will be hated by society if we follow Jesus. Have you experienced this? If so, describe your experience.

    c. "Remember the word that I said to you, 'A servant is not greater than his master.' If they persecuted Me, they will also persecute you. If they kept My word, they will keep yours also" (v. 20). Jesus promises we *will* be persecuted. When you are doing what is right— what is moral and biblical, you will face opposition and persecution, and the cost may be great. How can we find encouragement in these verses?

d. What is our ultimate reward for remaining faithful followers of Christ?

Spend time in your group praying for each other to stay engaged in the current battles—no surrender, no retreat—and diligently prepare for future battles.

Get Recalibrated

It's not enough to know a battle is coming; you must also prepare for the fight. Just as the military trains, drills, and practices over and over in preparation for all foreseeable enemies and situations, we, too, are engaged in battle against a relentless enemy. We must not only prepare ourselves for the fight and inevitable persecutions, but we must also prepare those around us. No man fights alone!

Get Prepared

To prepare for the next session's reflection and discussion, read Chapter 16 and Jeremy Stalnecker's afterword, "Building a Wall."

SUIT UP IN THE ARMOR OF GOD

Get Ready

Read the following:

- Chapter 16: Courage Beyond Fear

Get Focused

The way we understand and experience both fear and risk changes with time. That is, our fears as children are starkly different from our fears as adults. The same is true with risk: some of us grow more cautious with age, and some of us become bold and daring. A significant element to our biblical manhood is how we handle these aspects of life.

Get in the Fight

When we're young, we tend to believe we're invincible. The possibility that we could get hurt or even die during our wild activities just didn't occur to us as young men. In instances of sustained exposure to the risks, we often recognize the danger but choose to ignore it. As Chad said concerning his life-threatening missions, "But the very real possibility that I might be only moments away

from these fears becoming reality weighed heavily against the bravado that I was somehow immune to these dangers."

1. Discuss times in your life when you recognized a significant risk associated with whatever you were doing. What did it take for you to finally acknowledge the risk?

2. Sometimes, risk comes with doing what we believe to be a greater good, but prolonged exposure to this kind of risk can be exhausting and devastating.

    a. Did acknowledging the risk lead to subsequent fear?

    b. How did you mitigate that fear?

    c. Did you share your fears with others close to you?

3. Chad talks about living with this kind of fear and that "regardless of our personal fear, we press forward in the belief that the price of the sacrifice is worth the cost." What is within us that often makes us push forward despite great personal risk?

4. Chapter 16 addresses numerous warriors and their mighty deeds, but the most impressive warrior of all was Jesus Christ. How have you pictured Jesus in your mind? Was he the "wimpy, peace-love-and-happiness guy skipping around Jerusalem with a white robe and beautiful flowing hair," or do you picture him as a tough and courageous warrior who walked

boldly into unimaginable torture, humiliation, and death for the sake of everyone else's sake?

5. What was Jesus' unfair advantage, which is the same unfair advantage that's available to us, during his life, ministry, and death?

6. Fear often comes with uncertainty of the unknown. Have you ever experienced fear as a result of knowing in advance what would take place?

    a. Jesus knew exactly what would happen to him. Imagine knowing every detail of your impending betrayal, arrest, torture, and death. Why do you think this knowledge did not cause Jesus to become fearful?

    b. How is it easier, but not easy, to walk into difficult and potentially lengthy seasons and circumstances with an understanding that there will be victory?

7. Chad writes, "Courage is not the absence of fear but rather the decision that something is more important than that fear and moving on anyway." List at least three things that are more important than our fears.

    1. _____

    2. _____

    3. _____

Spend time in your group praying for each other to have the courage to continually pursue authentic biblical manhood and servant leadership despite our fears.

Get Recalibrated

Jesus had the unfair advantage of knowing the future. He knew he is God, and he knew his mission on earth. That knowledge would likely be too much for any of us to bear, but he moved forward courageously on our behalf. His example is one that we can and should strive to emulate during our challenging seasons of life. He has shown us how to suit-up in the full armor of God and how to live our lives with an unfair advantage.

Get Prepared

To prepare for the battles that lie ahead with an unfair advantage, we need to have a personal relationship with Jesus Christ. What's keeping you from claiming an unfair advantage and living with purpose?

Go Forth and Do Likewise

You have your battle orders. Your mission is clear, and it's twofold: it's time to rebuild your section of God's wall of restoration and at the same time pay it forward. Put what you learned here into practice. Set your course to greater authentic biblical manhood. And, as God uses this discussion guide and the time you spent going through it with your group to heal your hurts and restore the broken pieces, be vigilant in seeking opportunities to use your personal experiences, both good and bad, as a means to help others find their God-given purpose. Isolation is a path that leads to desolation. Invest in people and start with the ones God has already placed in your life.

Will there be resistance to the good you are doing in your life and in the lives of others? Of course. You're engaged in a battle. Remember Nehemiah and how he was not moved by the efforts to destroy him or his great work. Remember Chad and the Mighty Oaks story of success even as others try to pull his focus from his mission. They ignored the distractions and the opposition and pushed forward toward their goal. You, too, can join Nehemiah and Chad in your great work of restoration and declare, "I am carrying on a great project and cannot go down. Why should the work stop while I leave it and go down to you?"

As you re-enter the battlefield, keep in mind that God used Chad's story and the stories of the members of your study group to begin to rebuild and restore you. Now you have the responsibility to leverage your story of restoration to help others. Are you still a work in progress? Yes. We all are. But never forget that God, your Commander-in-Chief, has issued you your primary weapon: an unfair advantage!

Bibliography

1   Bridges, Jerry. *Trusting God*. United States: The Navigators, 2016.

2   *Spider-Man*, directed by Sam Raimi (2002; Los Angeles, CA: Sony Pictures Releasing, 2002), DVD.

3   Schorn, Daniel. "Mixed Martial Arts: A New Kind Of Fight." CBS News. CBS Interactive, December 8, 2006. https://www.cbsnews.com/news/mixed-martial-arts-a-new-kind-of-fight/.

4   Harold Myra and Marshall Shelley, *The Leadership Secrets of Billy Graham*, (Zondervan, 2005), 164.

CHAD ROBICHAUX
SPEAKING ENGAGEMENTS

- CORPORATE OUTINGS
- CHURCH SERVICES & EVENTS
- MILITARY EVENTS
- RESILIENCY CONFERENCES
- MEN'S EVENTS

CHAD HAS A PASSION TO SHARE THE
TRANSFORMATIONAL EXPERIENCE THAT CHANGED HIS
LIFE AND UNVEILED HIS PURPOSE.

CHAD'S PRESENTATIONS ON THE FOLLOWING TOPICS
ARE BOTH INSPIRING AND CHALLENGING AND CAN
BE SCALED FROM A SINGLE SESSION TO
MULTI-DAY/SESSION RETREATS AND CONFERENCES:

- MANHOOD   - LEGACY   - RESILIENCY
    - LEADERSHIP   - CHARACTER
    - LIVING A PURPOSEFUL LIFE

CHADROBICHAUX.COM